DISNEP
HANNAH MONTANA™

Based on the television series, "Hannah Montana,"
Created By
Michael Poryes and Rich Correll & Barry O'Brien

SECRETS AND SUPER SNEAKS

"Lilly, Do You Want to Know a Secret?"
Written By Steven Peterman, Gary Dontzig
and Michael Poryes

"She's a Super Sneak"
Written By Kim Friese

Editor - Julie Taylor
Contributing Editor - Marion Brown
Graphic Designer and Letterer - Anna Kernbaum
Cover Designer - Monalisa J. de Asis
Graphic Artist - Monalisa J. de Asis

Production Manager - Elisabeth Brizzi
Art Director - Anne Marie Horne
VP of Production - Ron Klamert
Editor in Chief - Rob Tokar
Publisher - Mike Kiley
President & C.O.O. - John Parker
C.E.O. & Chief Creative Officer - Stuart Levy

E-mail: info@TOKYOPOP.com
Come visit us online at www.TOKYOPOP.com

A ⊚ TOKYOPOP₈ Cine-Manga® Book
TOKYOPOP Inc.
5900 Wilshire Blvd., Suite 2000
Los Angeles, CA 90036

Hannah Montana Volume 1
© 2007 Disney

ISBN: 978-1-4278-0777-9

First TOKYOPOP® printing: July 2007

10 9 8 7 6 5 4 3 2 1

Printed in the USA

Disney

HANNAH MONTANA™

SECRETS AND SUPER SNEAKS

CONTENTS

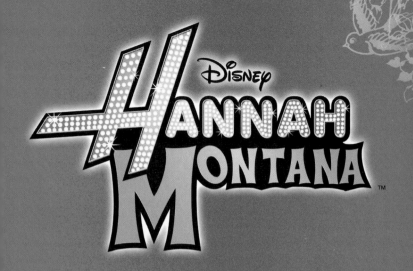

WHO'S WHO

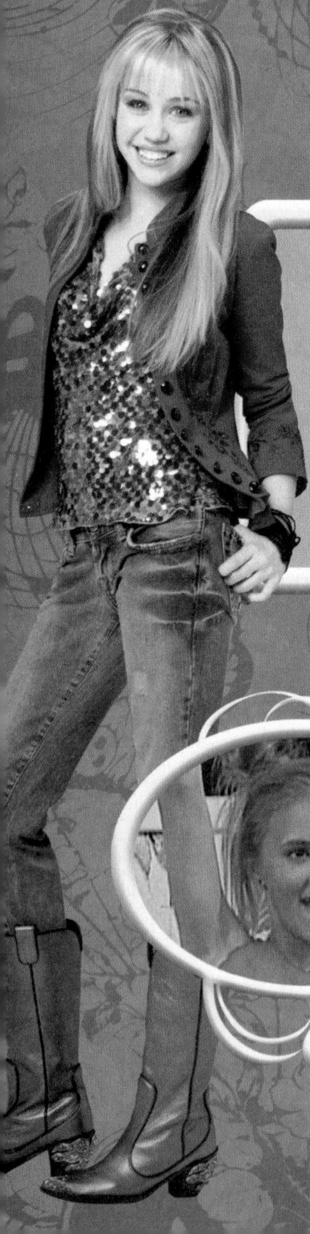

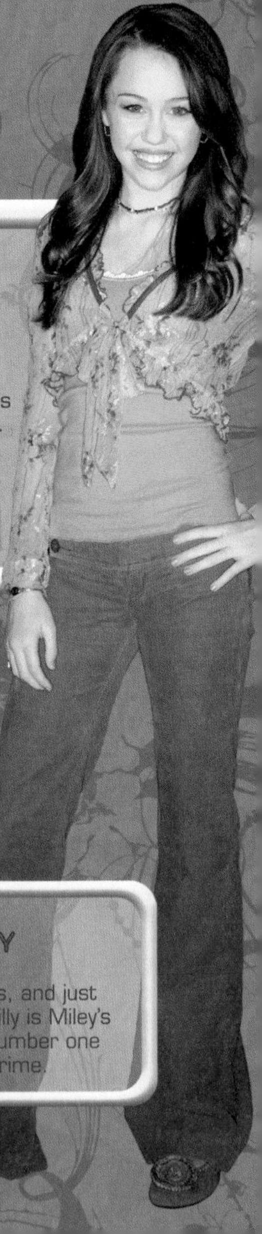

HANNAH MONTANA/ MILEY

She's the girl next door who just so happens to moonlight as a world-famous pop sensation. But underneath the glamour of a superstar, Miley Stewart is a regular girl who gets into all kinds of sticky situations.

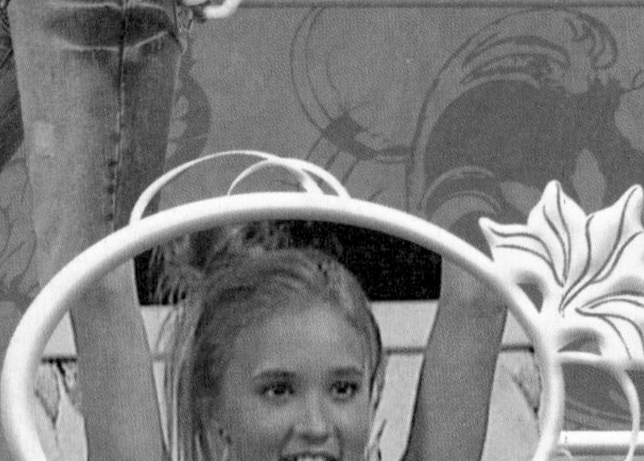

LILLY

Fun, spontaneous, and just a little bit wacky, Lilly is Miley's best friend and number one partner in crime.

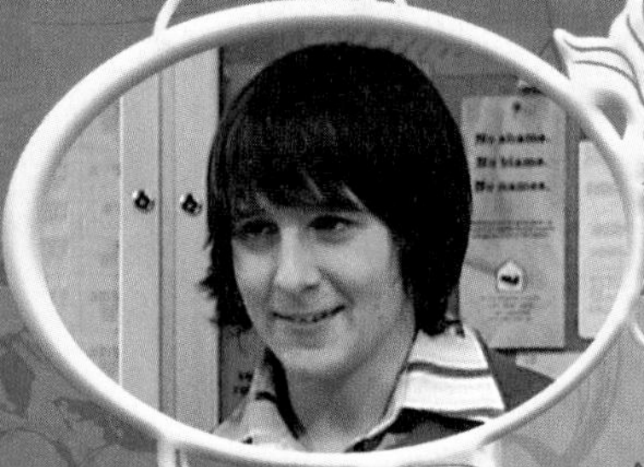

OLIVER

A super-cool goofball, Oliver is a good friend of both Miley and Lilly.

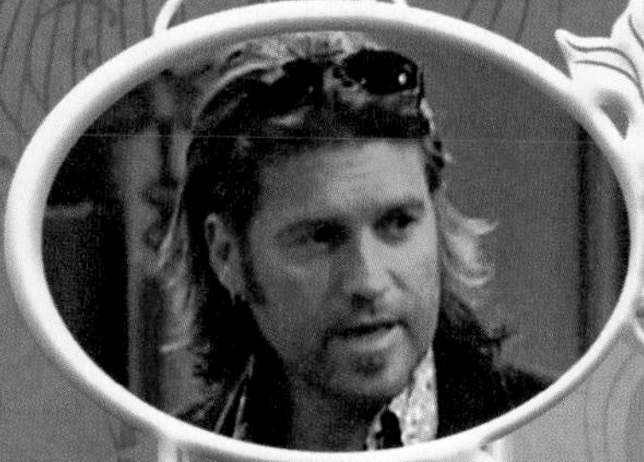

ROBBY

Miley's dad is a country musician who knows enough about showbiz to keep his little girl, the pop star, rock solid.

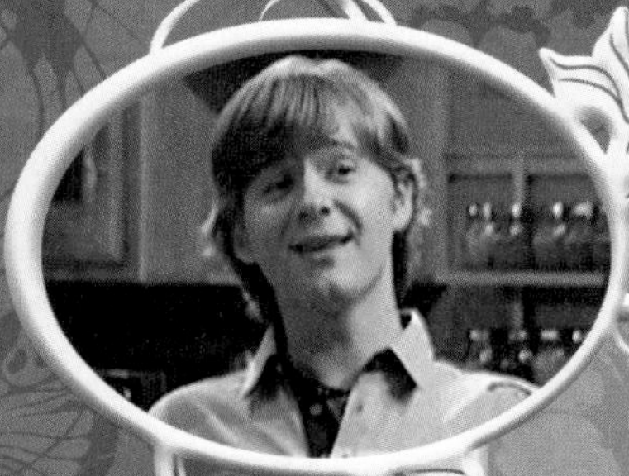

JACKSON

More silly than slick, Miley's brother Jackson definitely has his own way of doing things.

"LILLY, DO YOU WANT TO KNOW A SECRET?"

SECRET CELEBRI

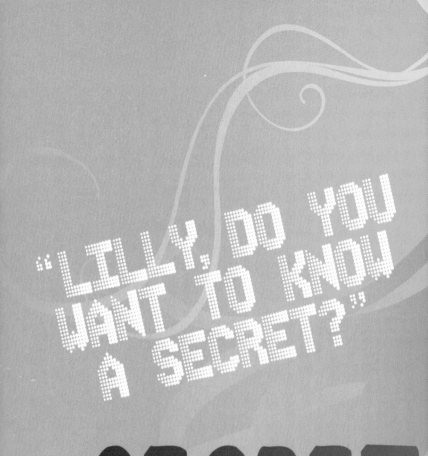

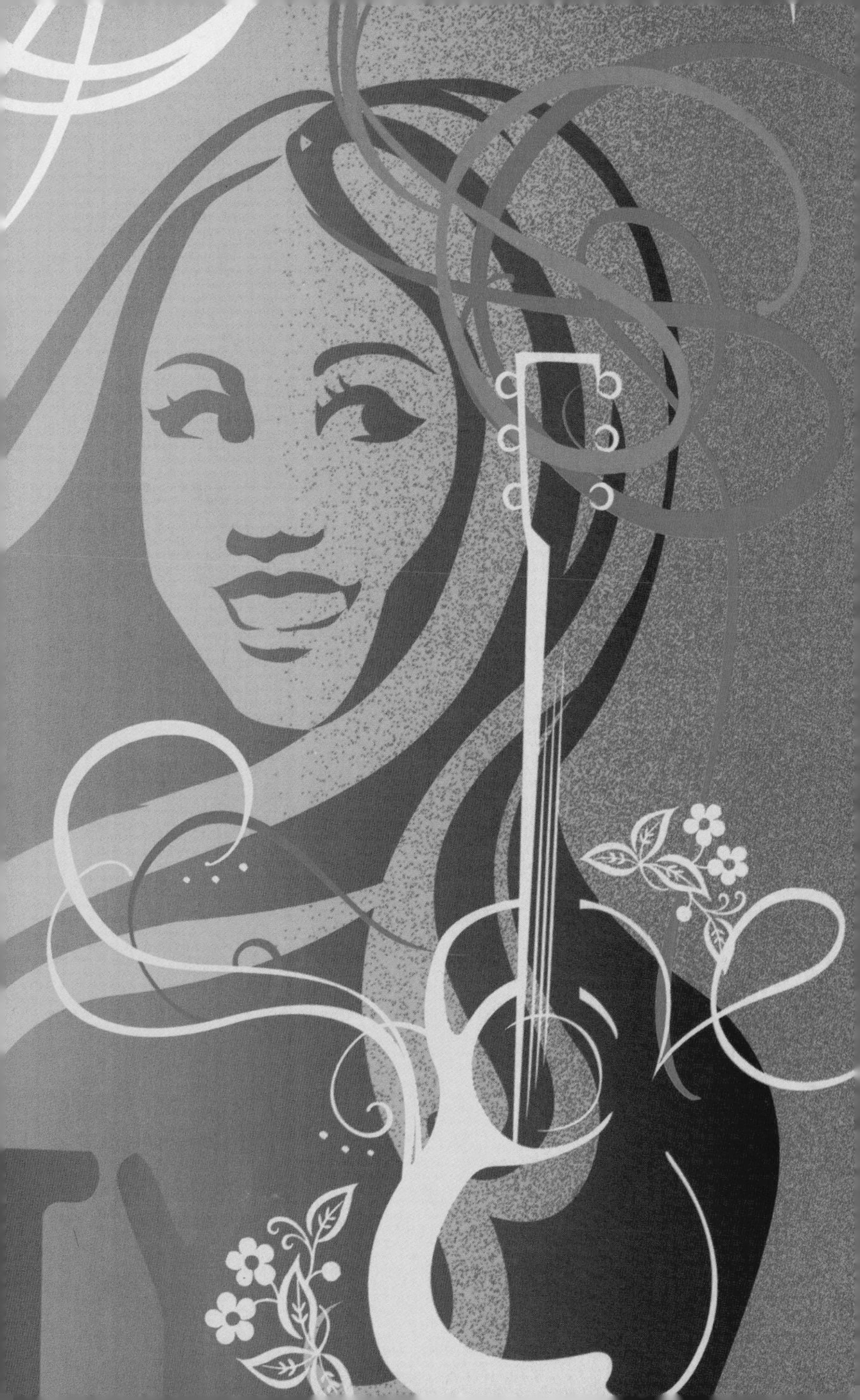

FROM HANNAH'S LATEST MUSIC VIDEO...

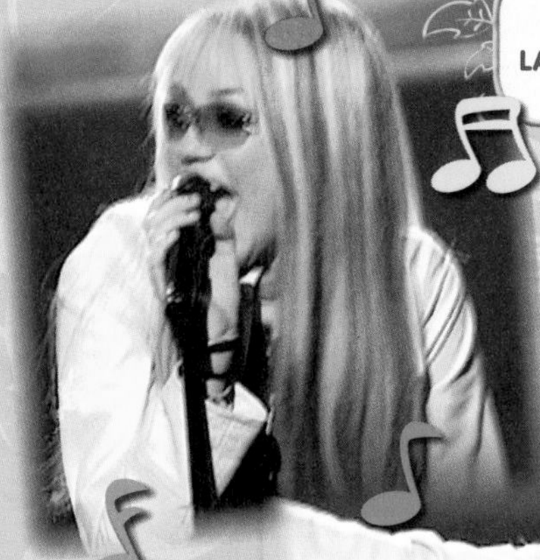

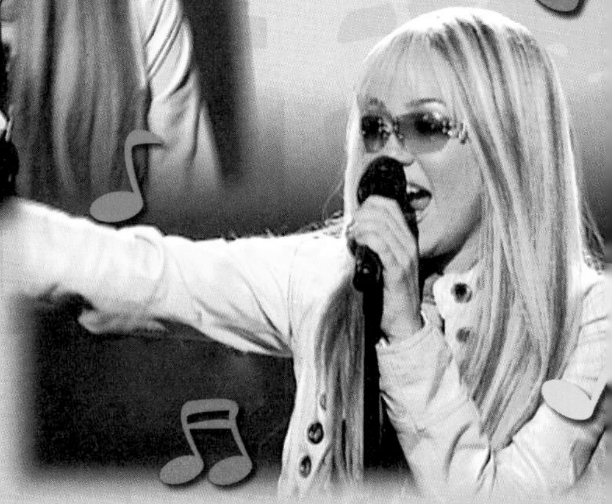

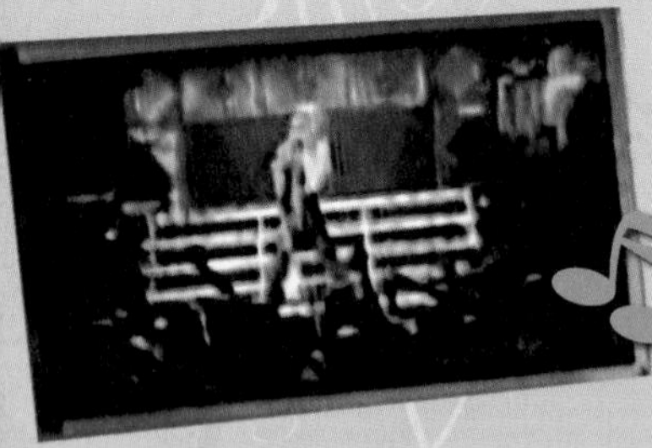

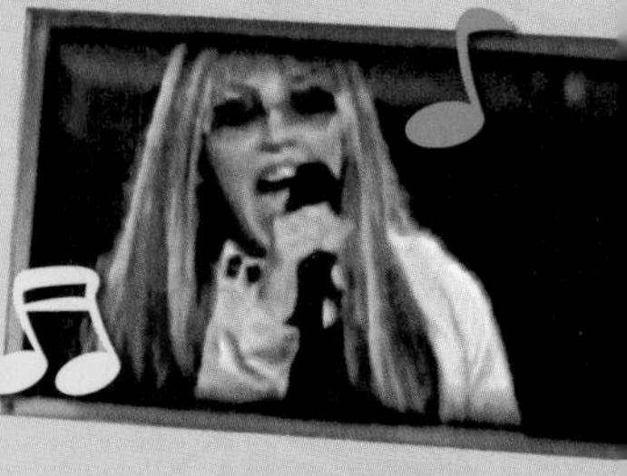

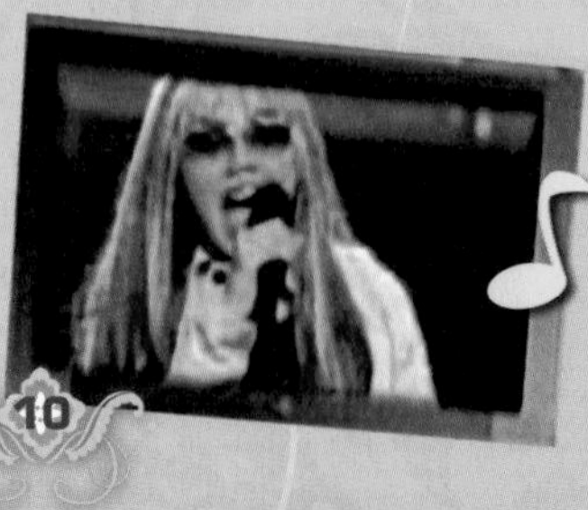

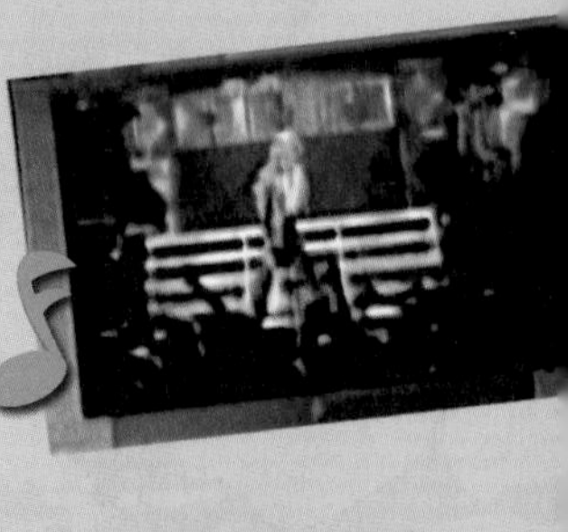

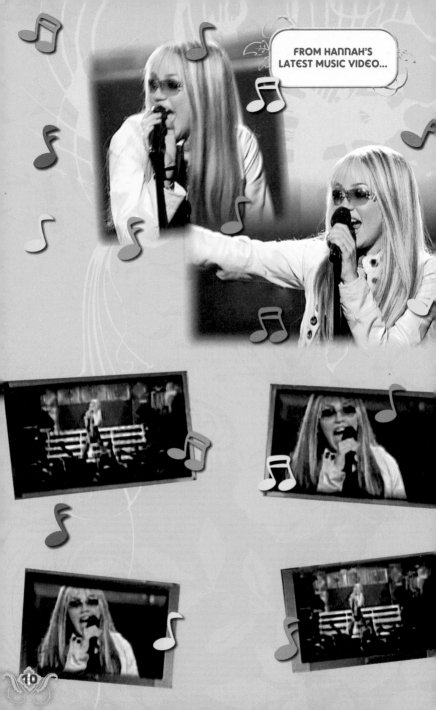

IN MILEY'S KITCHEN...

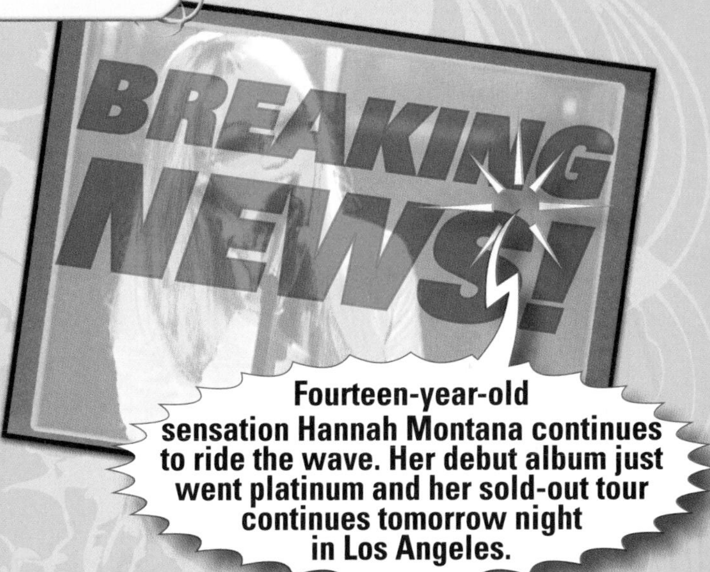
BREAKING NEWS!
Fourteen-year-old sensation Hannah Montana continues to ride the wave. Her debut album just went platinum and her sold-out tour continues tomorrow night in Los Angeles.

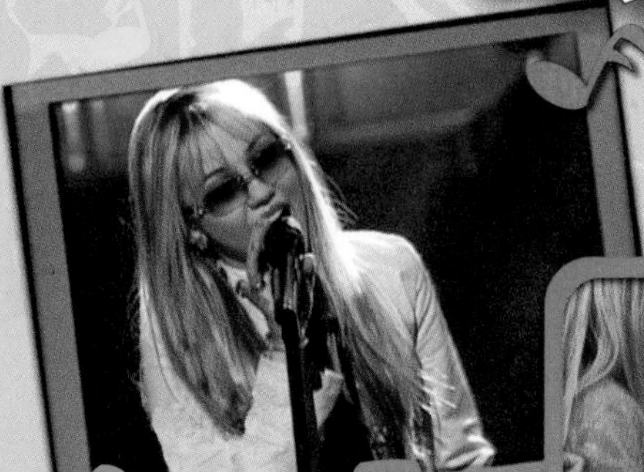

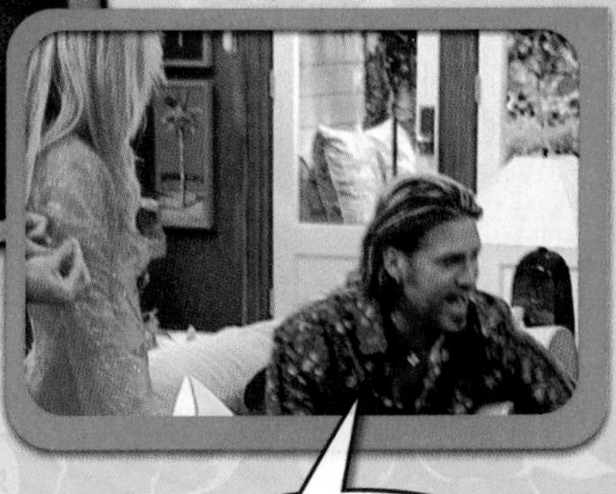
Hear that, superstar? Hannah Montana: Sold out in Los Angeles.

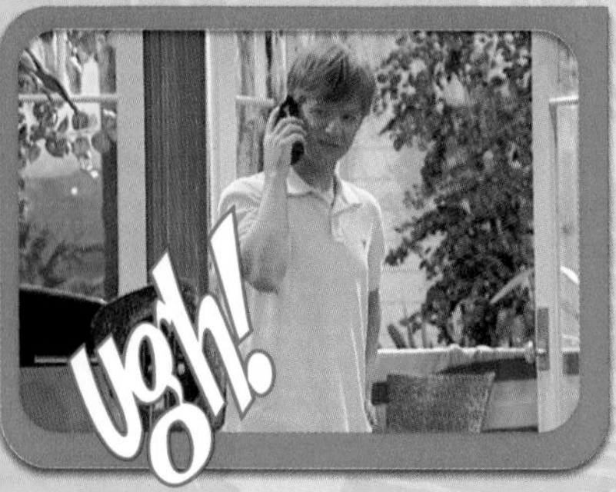
ugh!

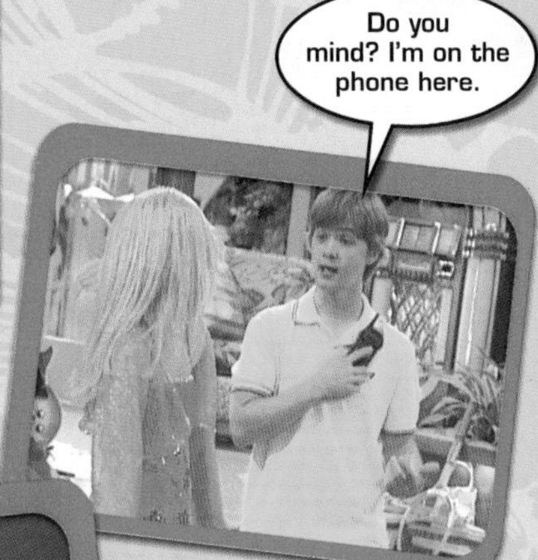
Do you mind? I'm on the phone here.

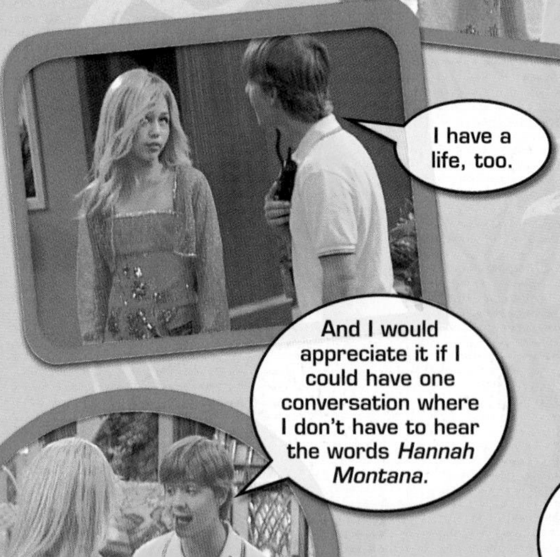
I have a life, too.

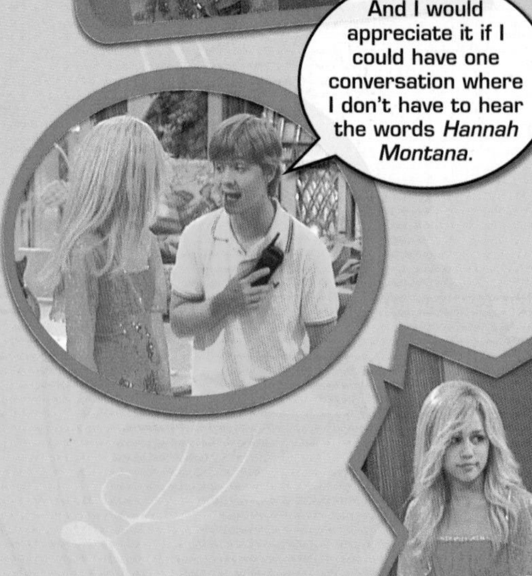
And I would appreciate it if I could have one conversation where I don't have to hear the words *Hannah Montana*.

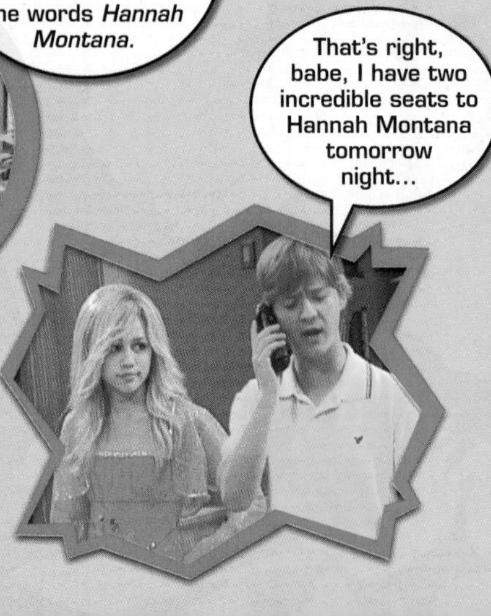
That's right, babe, I have two incredible seats to Hannah Montana tomorrow night...

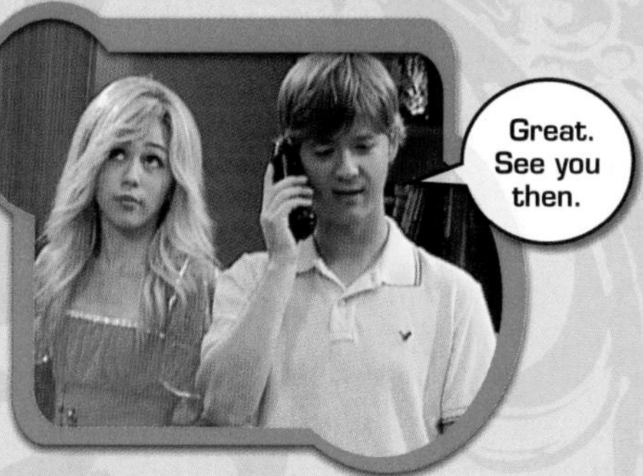
Great. See you then.
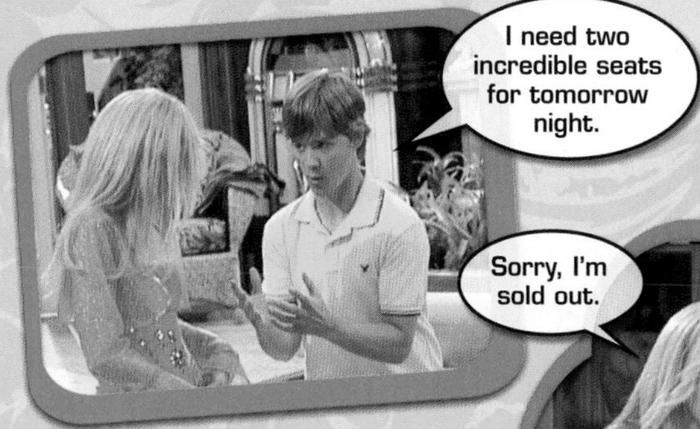
I need two incredible seats for tomorrow night.
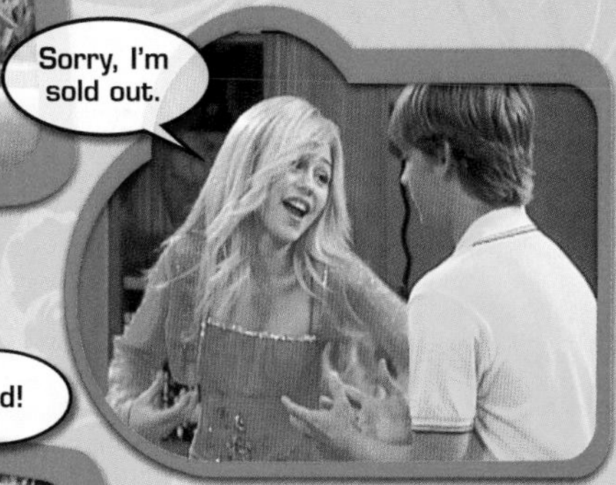
Sorry, I'm sold out.
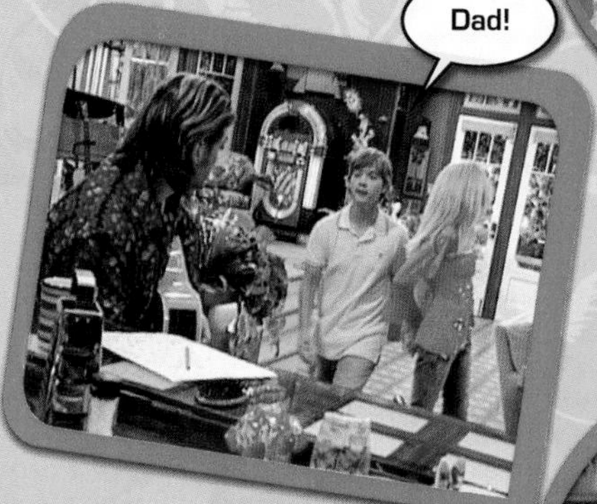
Dad!
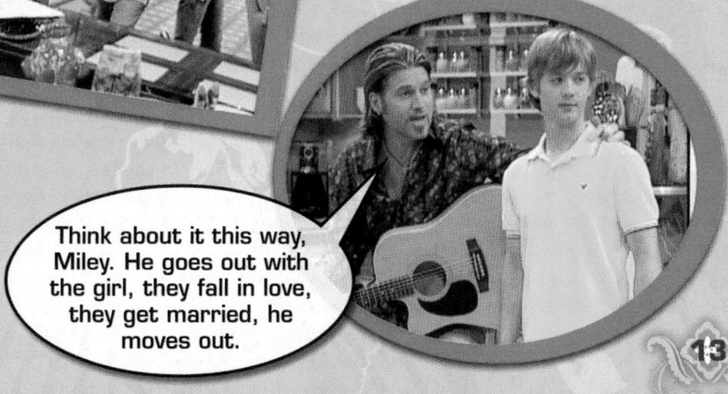
Think about it this way, Miley. He goes out with the girl, they fall in love, they get married, he moves out.

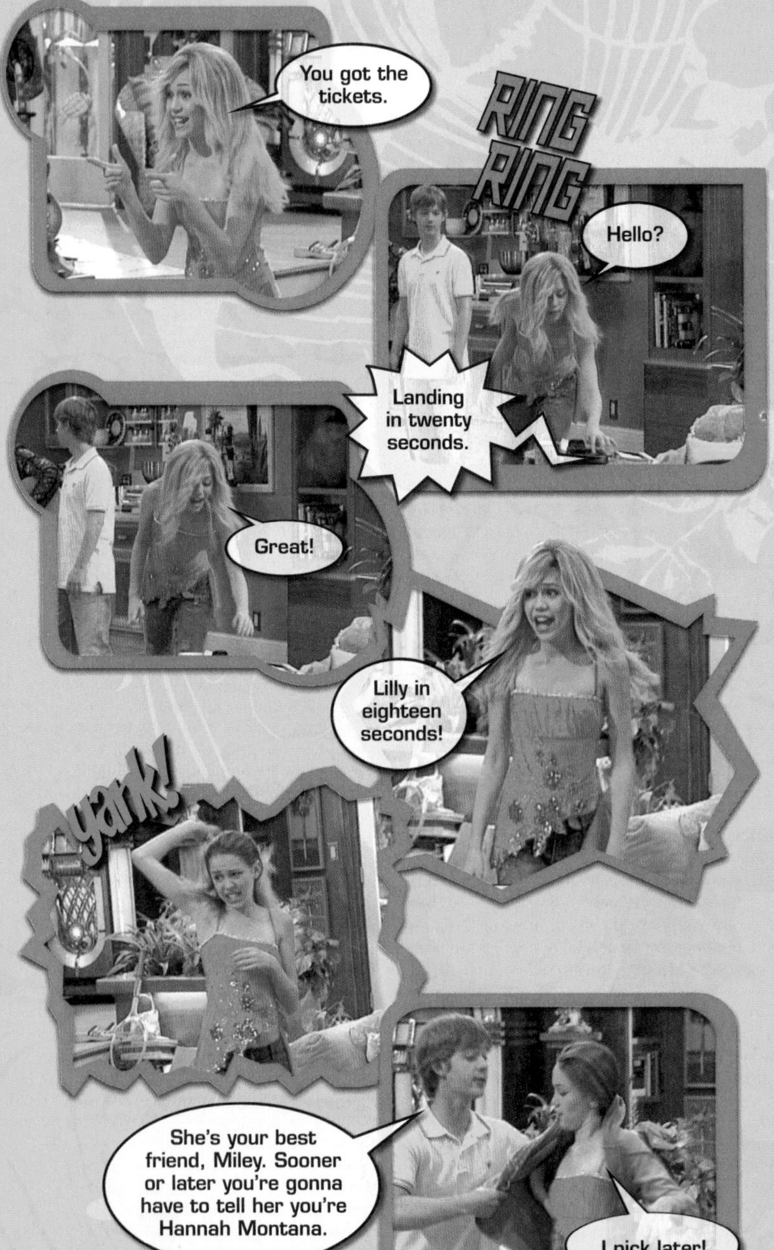
You got the tickets.
RING RING
Hello?
Landing in twenty seconds.
Great!
Lilly in eighteen seconds!
yank!
She's your best friend, Miley. Sooner or later you're gonna have to tell her you're Hannah Montana.
I pick later!

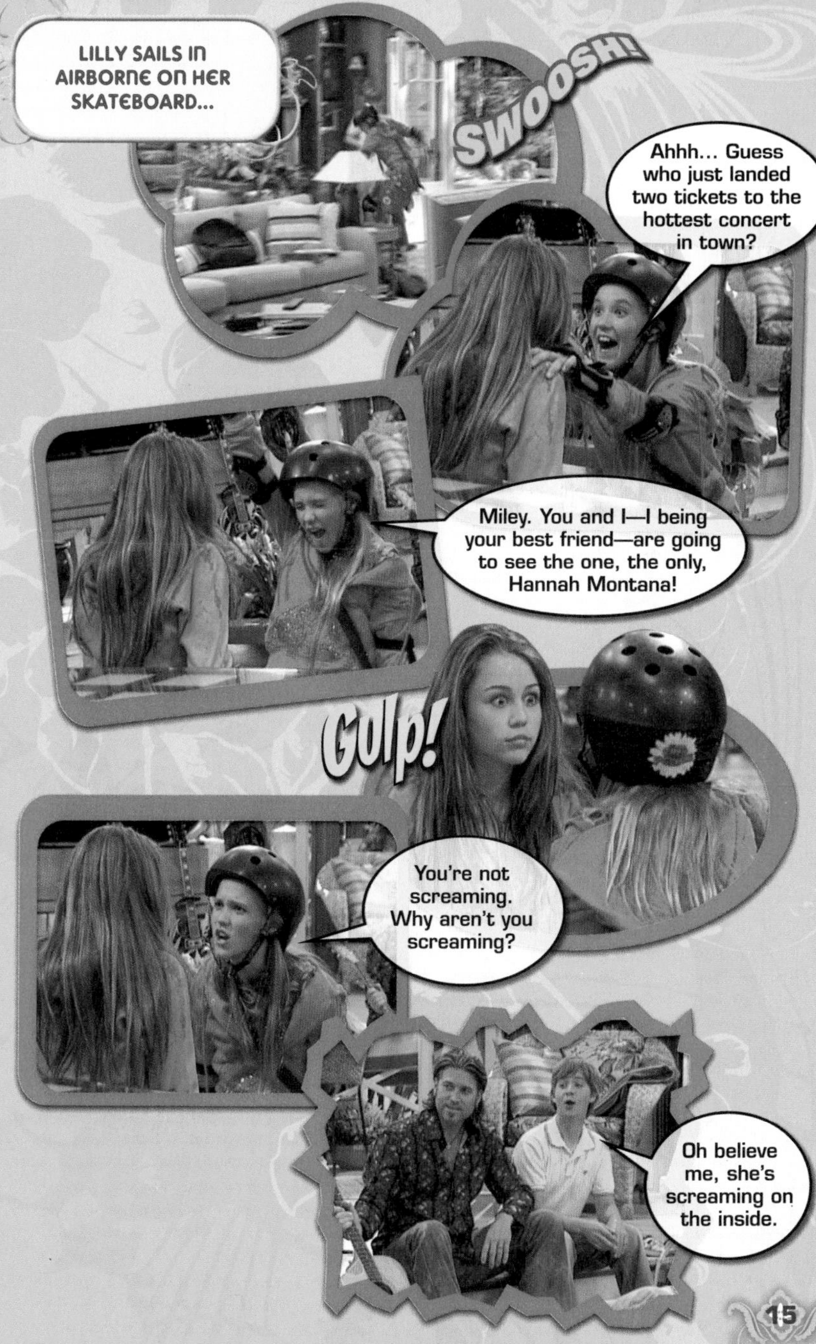
LILLY SAILS IN AIRBORNE ON HER SKATEBOARD...
SWOOSH!
Ahhh... Guess who just landed two tickets to the hottest concert in town?
Miley. You and I—I being your best friend—are going to see the one, the only, Hannah Montana!
Gulp!
You're not screaming. Why aren't you screaming?
Oh believe me, she's screaming on the inside.

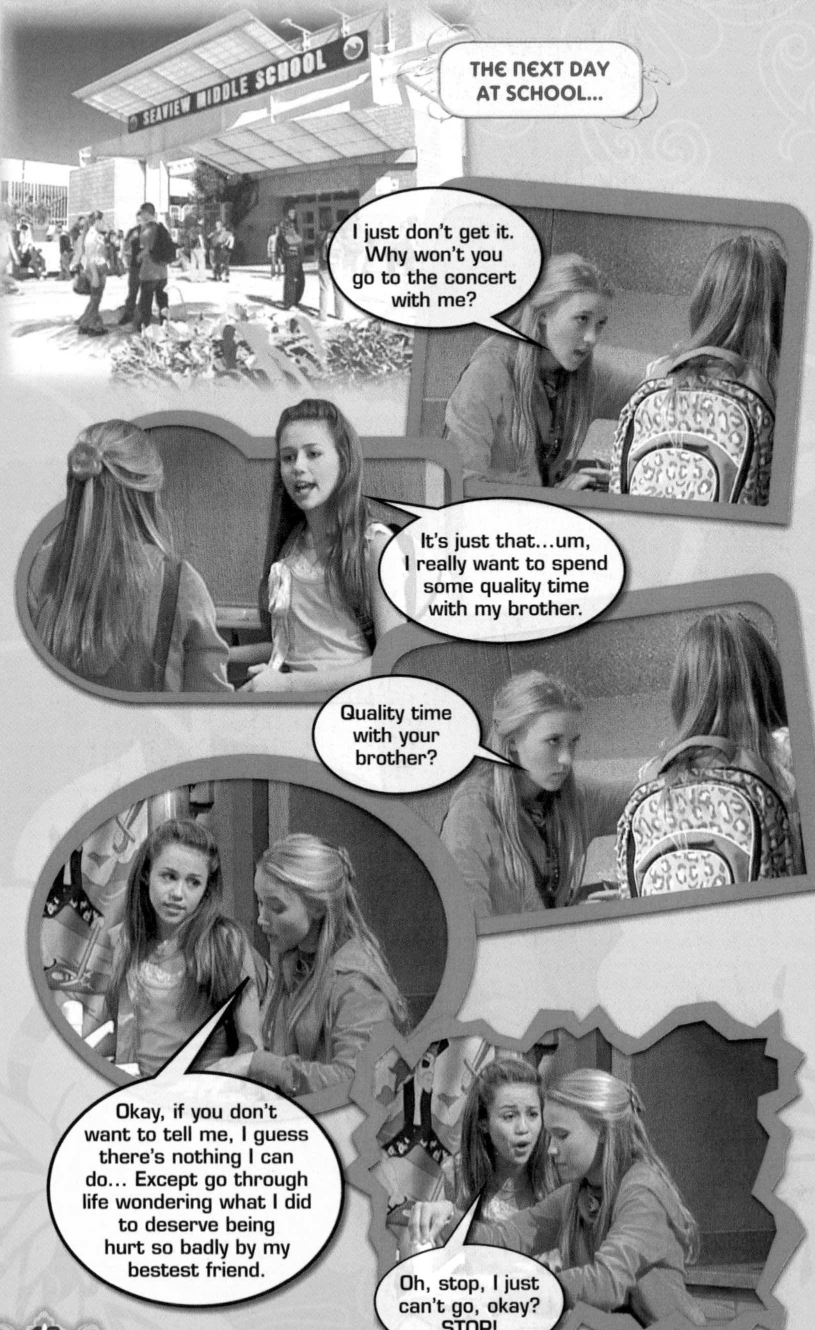
SEAVIEW MIDDLE SCHOOL
THE NEXT DAY AT SCHOOL...
I just don't get it. Why won't you go to the concert with me?
It's just that...um, I really want to spend some quality time with my brother.
Quality time with your brother?
Okay, if you don't want to tell me, I guess there's nothing I can do... Except go through life wondering what I did to deserve being hurt so badly by my bestest friend.
Oh, stop, I just can't go, okay? STOP!

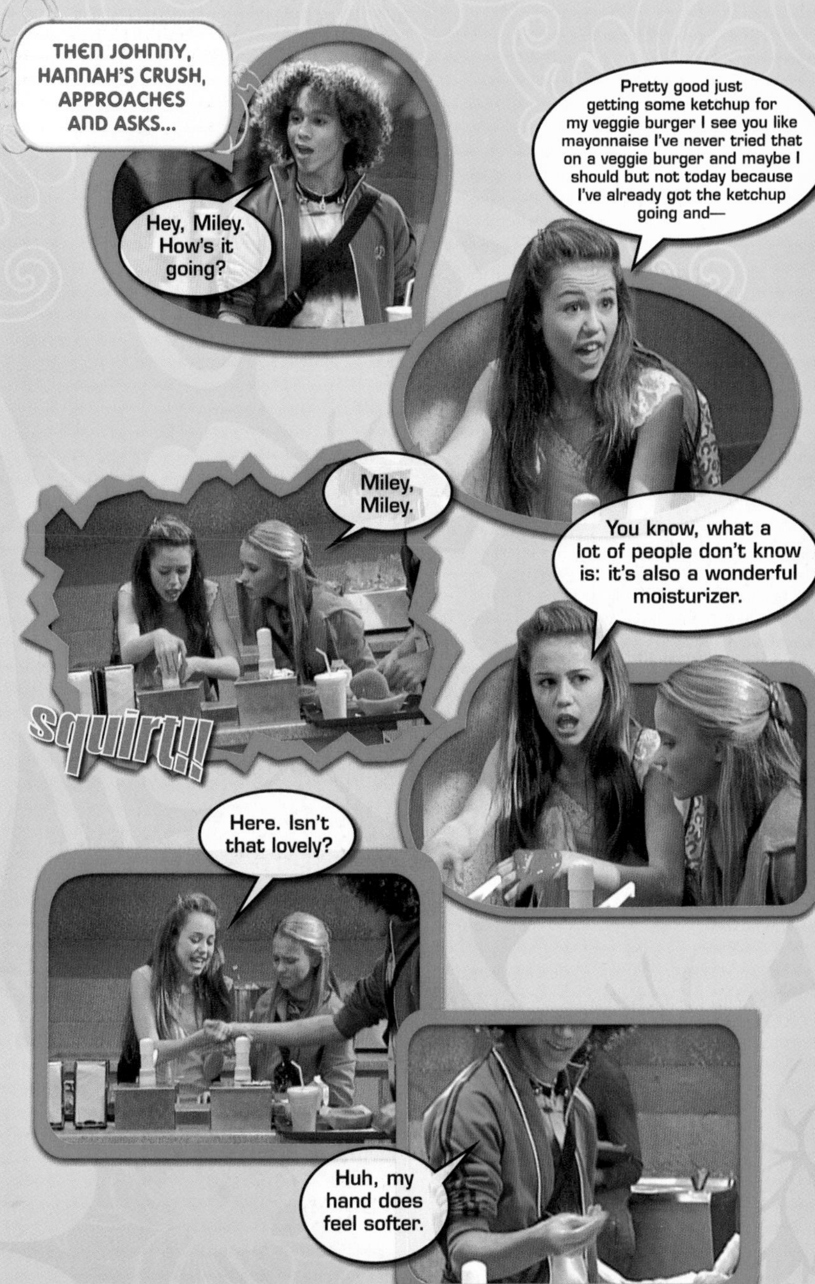
THEN JOHNNY, HANNAH'S CRUSH, APPROACHES AND ASKS...
Hey, Miley. How's it going?
Pretty good just getting some ketchup for my veggie burger I see you like mayonnaise I've never tried that on a veggie burger and maybe I should but not today because I've already got the ketchup going and—
Miley, Miley.
squirt!!
You know, what a lot of people don't know is: it's also a wonderful moisturizer.
Here. Isn't that lovely?
Huh, my hand does feel softer.

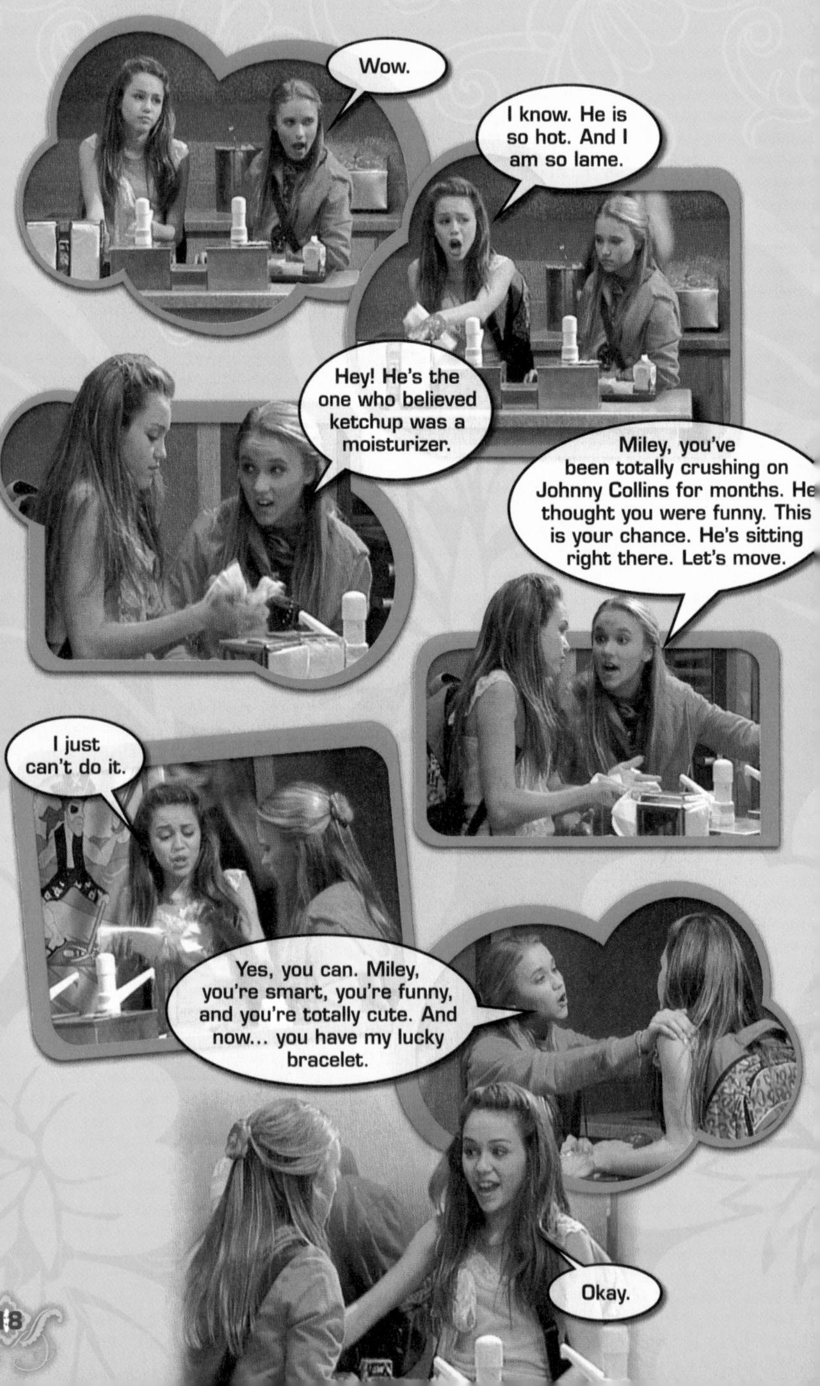
Wow.
I know. He is so hot. And I am so lame.
Hey! He's the one who believed ketchup was a moisturizer.
Miley, you've been totally crushing on Johnny Collins for months. He thought you were funny. This is your chance. He's sitting right there. Let's move.
I just can't do it.
Yes, you can. Miley, you're smart, you're funny, and you're totally cute. And now... you have my lucky bracelet.
Okay.

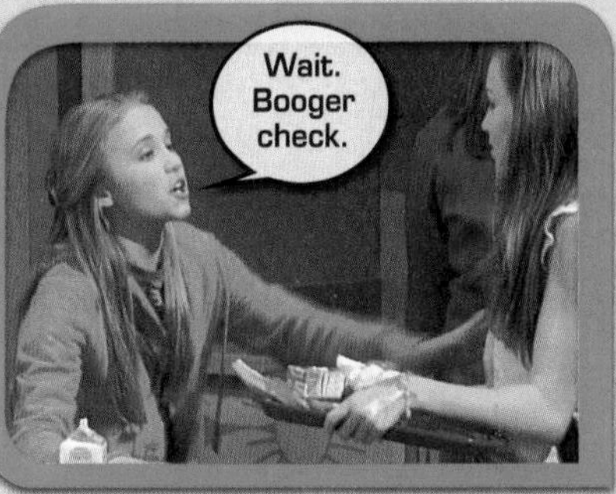
Wait. Booger check.

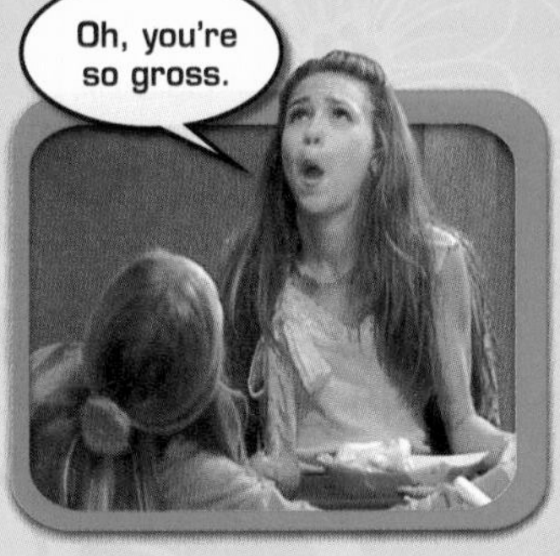
Oh, you're so gross.

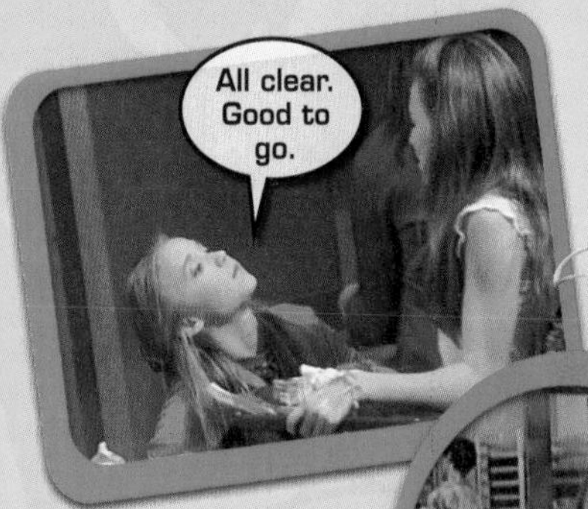
All clear. Good to go.

MILEY AND LILLY HEAD FOR THE SEATS RIGHT NEXT TO JOHNNY.

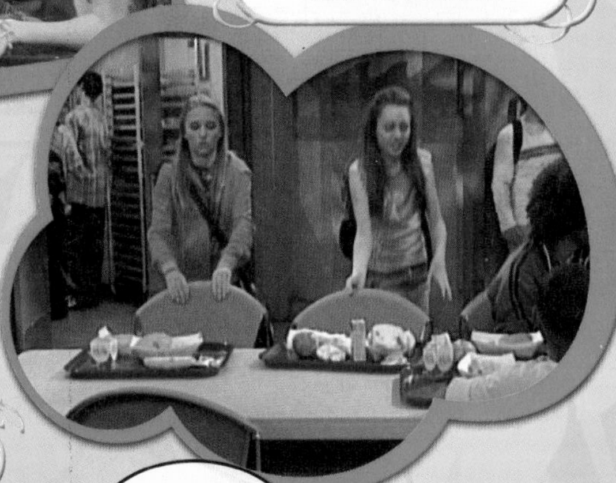

AMBER AND ASHLEY SLIP INTO MILEY AND LILLY'S SEATS.

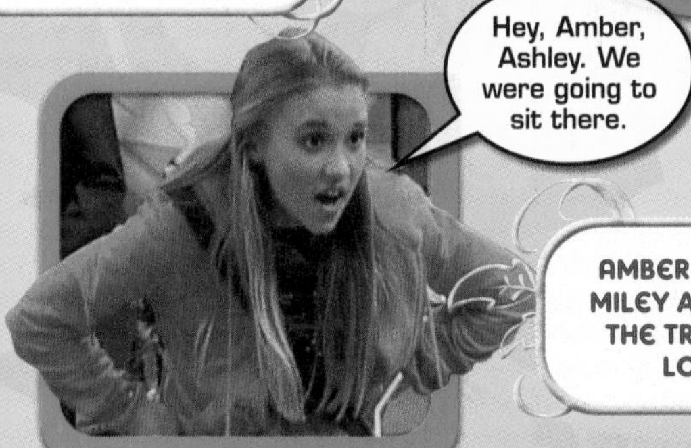
Hey, Amber, Ashley. We were going to sit there.

AMBER AND ASHLEY TELL MILEY AND LILLY TO SIT BY THE TRASH CANS AT THE LOSERS' TABLE!

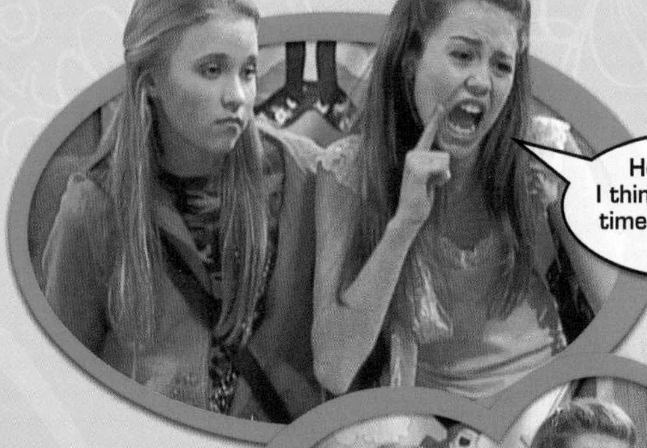
Hey Amber, I think it might be time to pluck the 'stache.

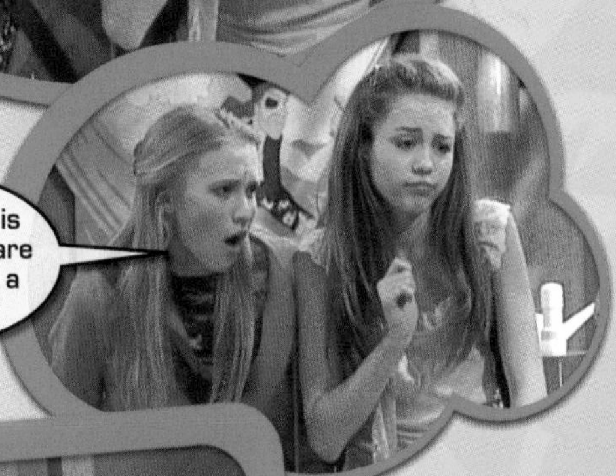
And Ashley, is that a zit or are you growing a new head?

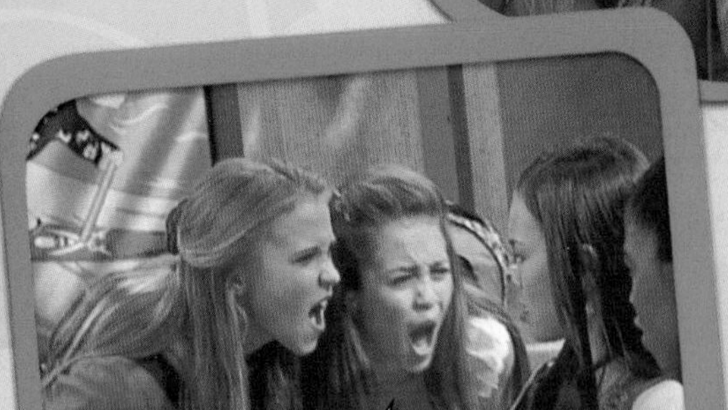
Gross!

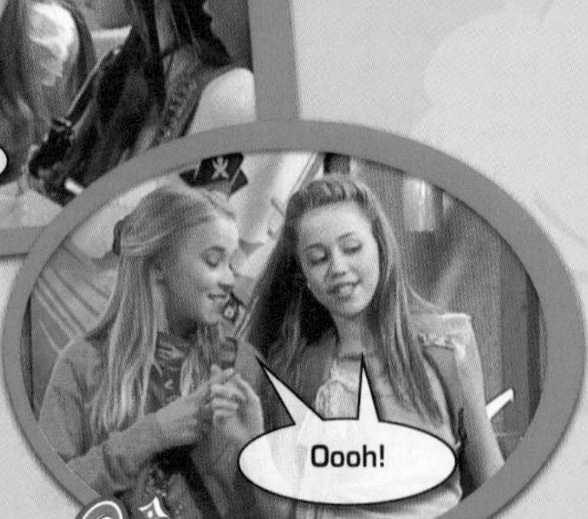
Oooh!

SIZZLE!

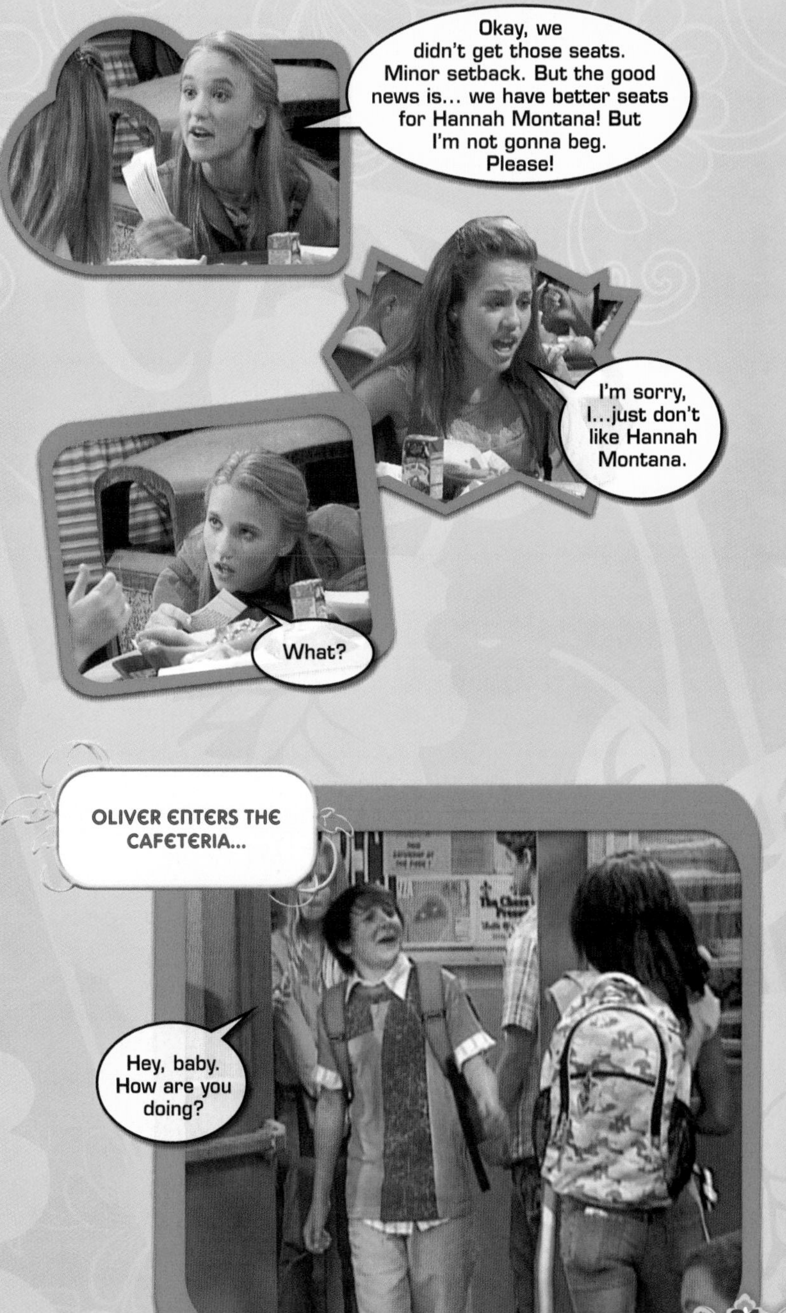
Okay, we didn't get those seats. Minor setback. But the good news is... we have better seats for Hannah Montana! But I'm not gonna beg. Please!
I'm sorry, I...just don't like Hannah Montana.
What?
OLIVER ENTERS THE CAFETERIA...
Hey, baby. How are you doing?

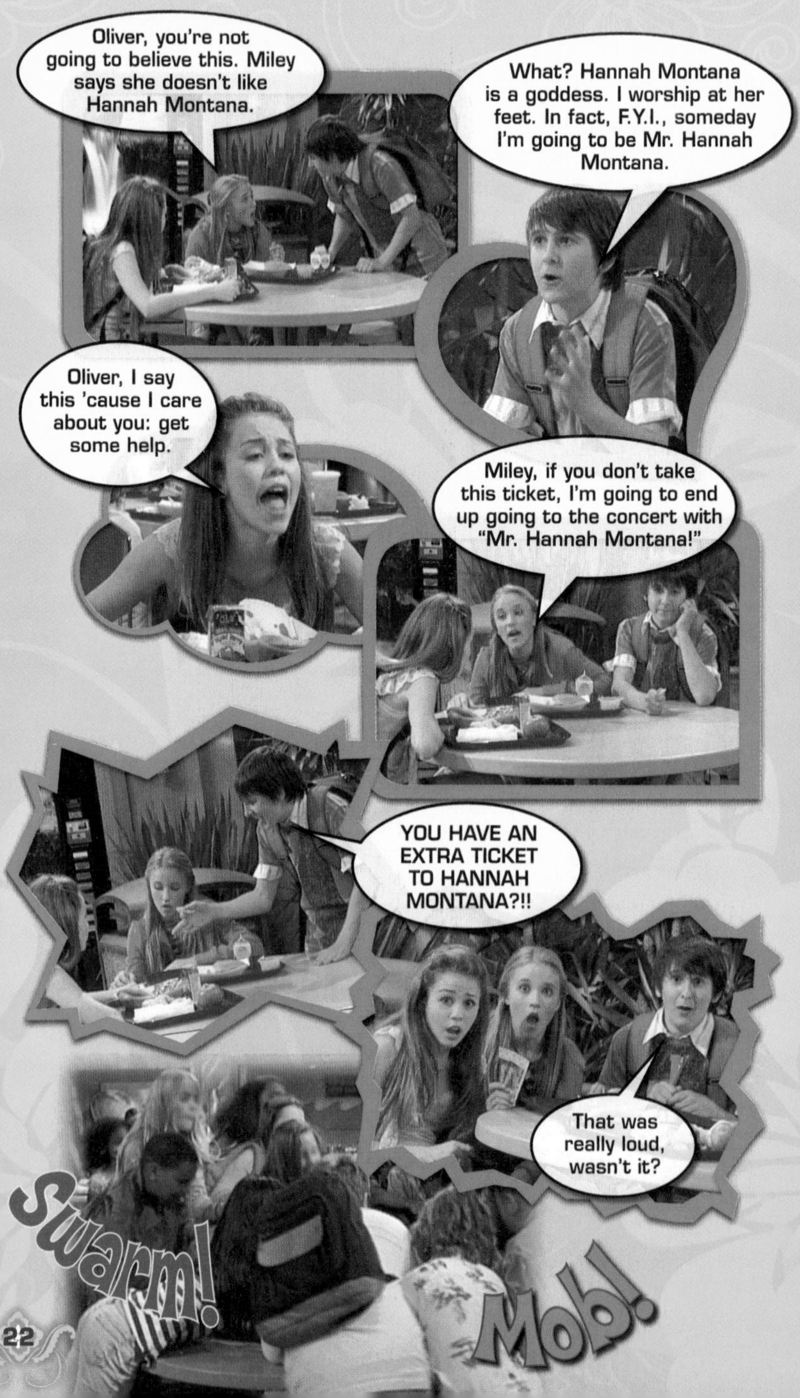
Oliver, you're not going to believe this. Miley says she doesn't like Hannah Montana.
What? Hannah Montana is a goddess. I worship at her feet. In fact, F.Y.I., someday I'm going to be Mr. Hannah Montana.
Oliver, I say this 'cause I care about you: get some help.
Miley, if you don't take this ticket, I'm going to end up going to the concert with "Mr. Hannah Montana!"
YOU HAVE AN EXTRA TICKET TO HANNAH MONTANA?!!
That was really loud, wasn't it?
Swarm!
Mob!

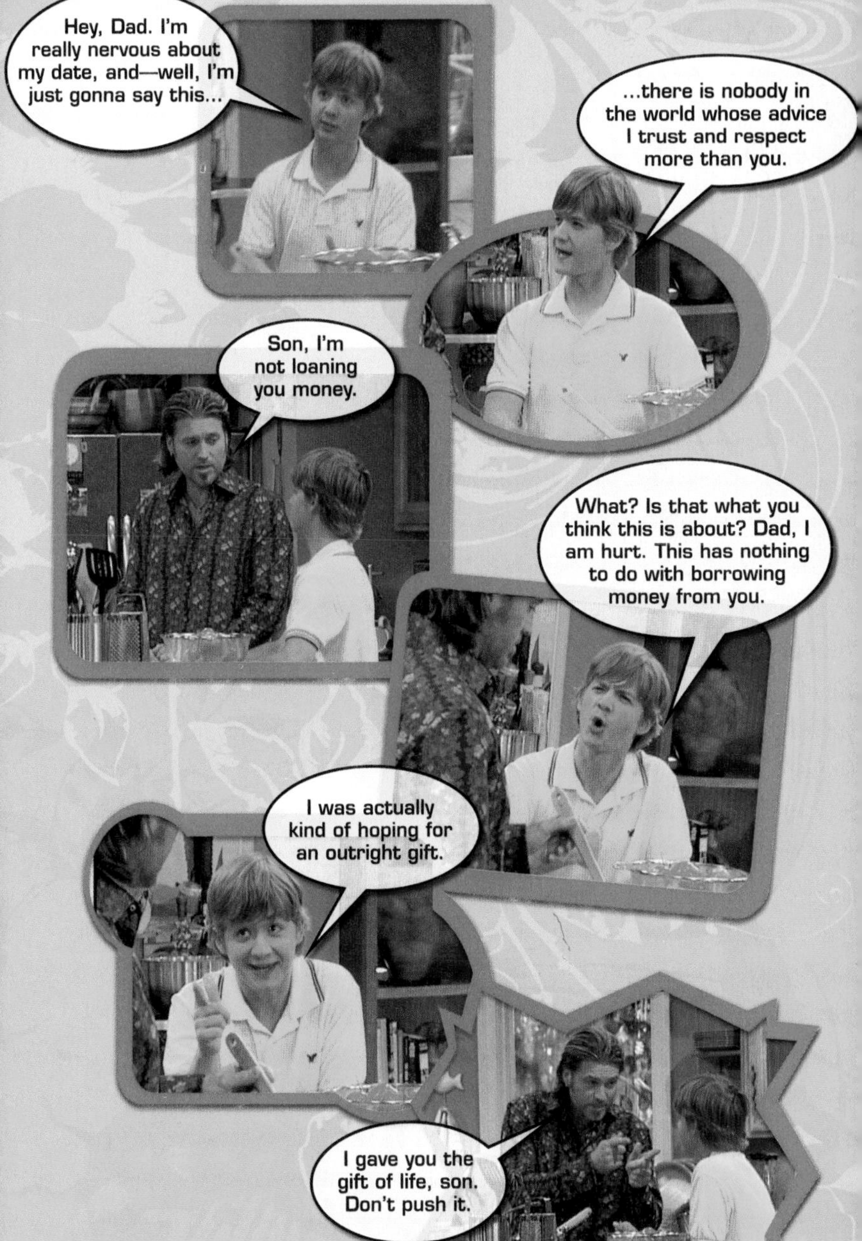
Hey, Dad. I'm really nervous about my date, and—well, I'm just gonna say this...
...there is nobody in the world whose advice I trust and respect more than you.
Son, I'm not loaning you money.
What? Is that what you think this is about? Dad, I am hurt. This has nothing to do with borrowing money from you.
I was actually kind of hoping for an outright gift.
I gave you the gift of life, son. Don't push it.

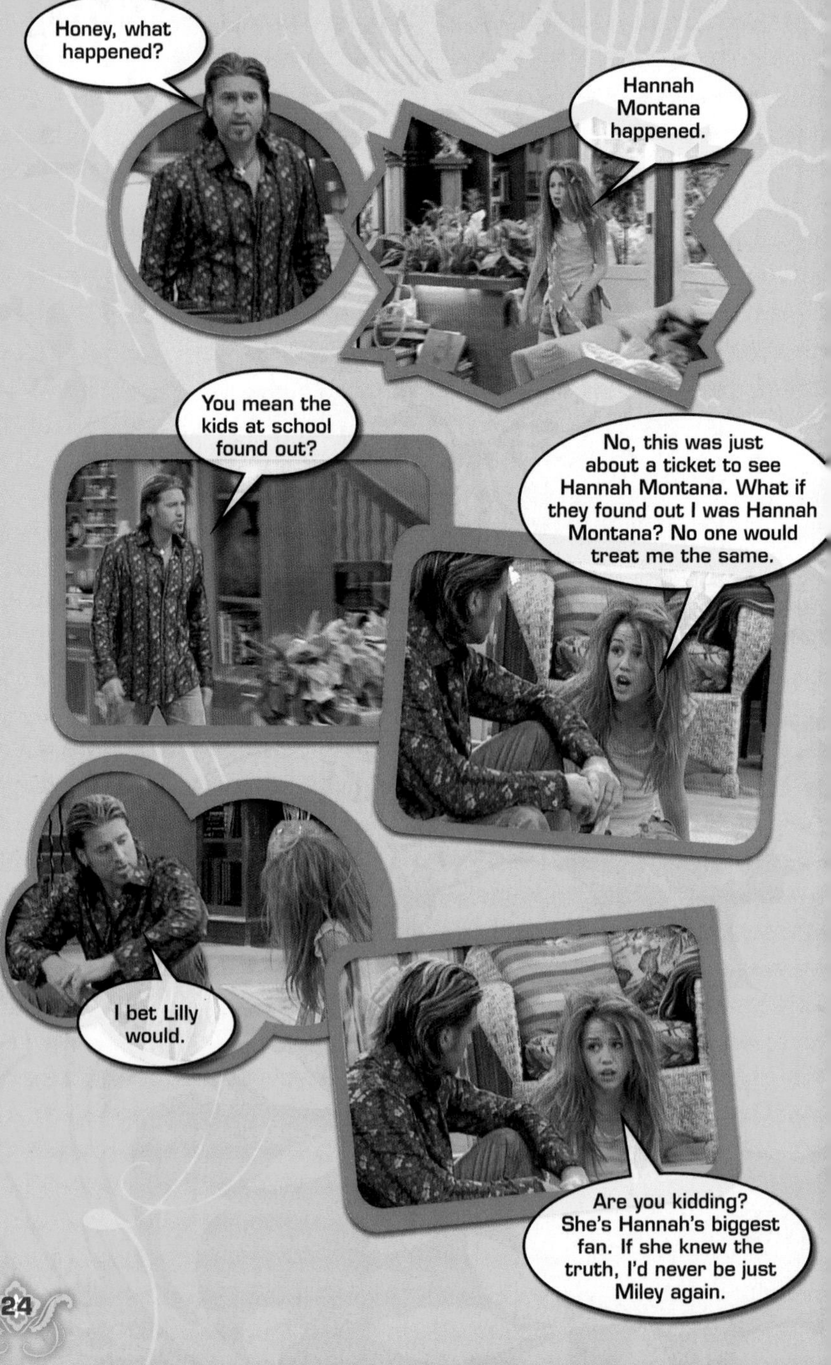

Honey, what happened?
Hannah Montana happened.
You mean the kids at school found out?
No, this was just about a ticket to see Hannah Montana. What if they found out I was Hannah Montana? No one would treat me the same.
I bet Lilly would.
Are you kidding? She's Hannah's biggest fan. If she knew the truth, I'd never be just Miley again.

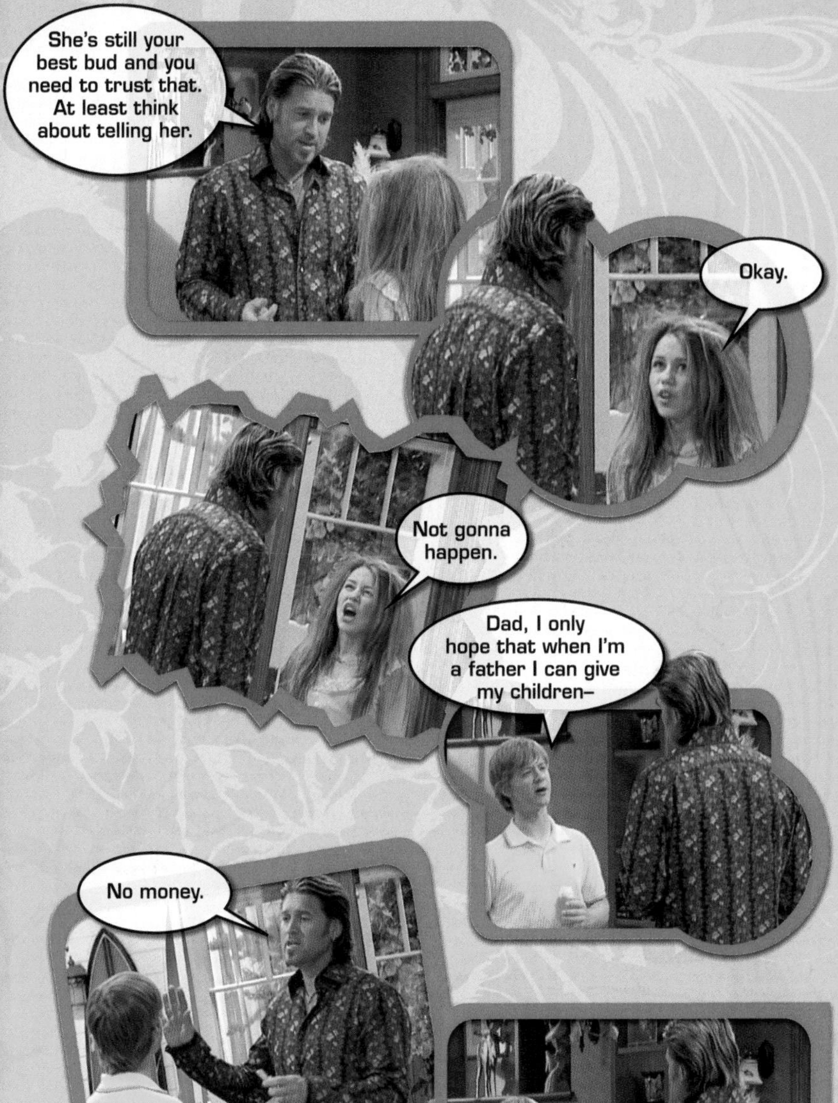
She's still your best bud and you need to trust that. At least think about telling her.
Okay.
Not gonna happen.
Dad, I only hope that when I'm a father I can give my children–
No money.
Didn't think so.

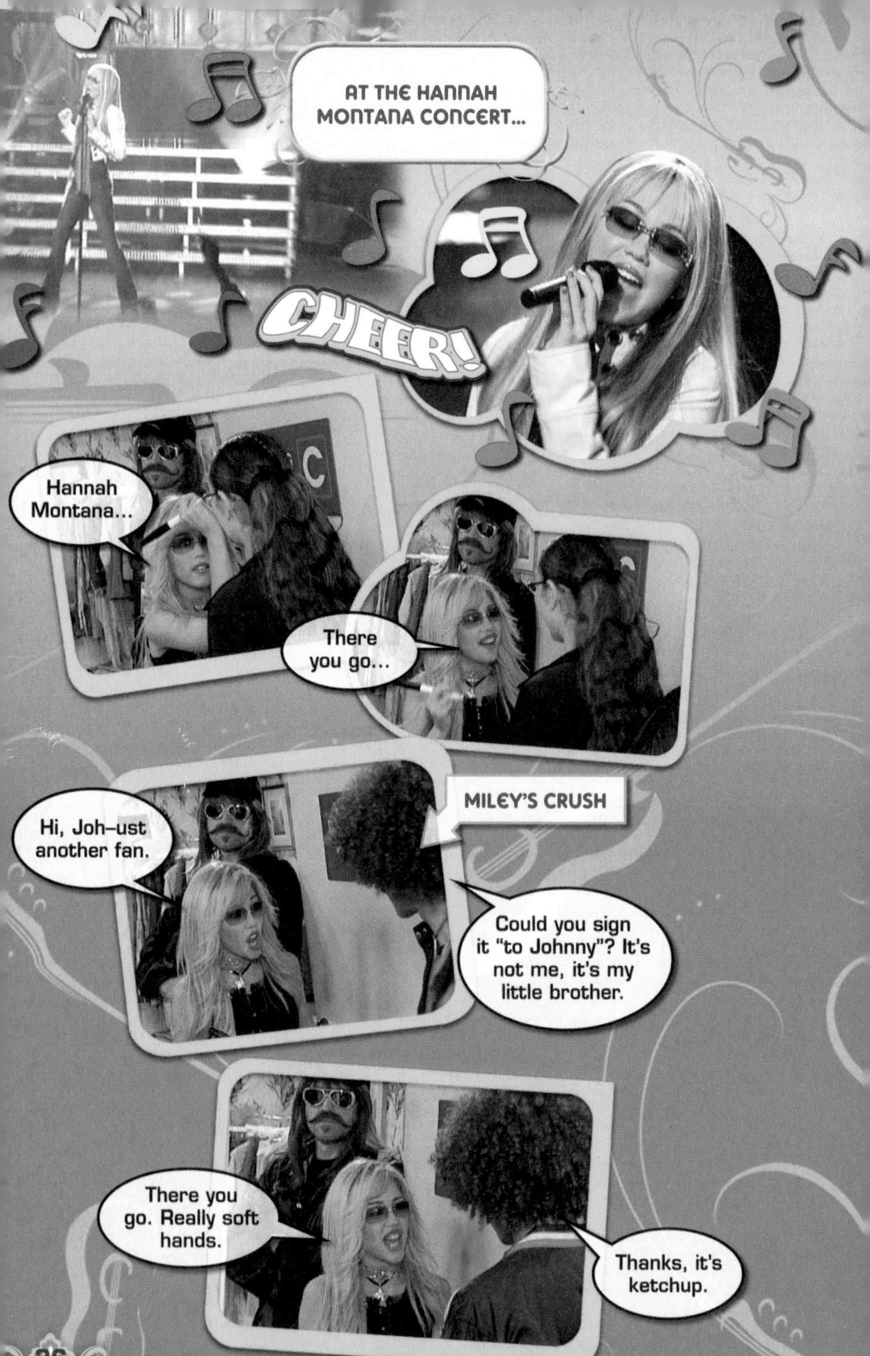
AT THE HANNAH MONTANA CONCERT...
CHEER!
Hannah Montana...
There you go...
Hi, Joh–ust another fan.
MILEY'S CRUSH
Could you sign it "to Johnny"? It's not me, it's my little brother.
There you go. Really soft hands.
Thanks, it's ketchup.

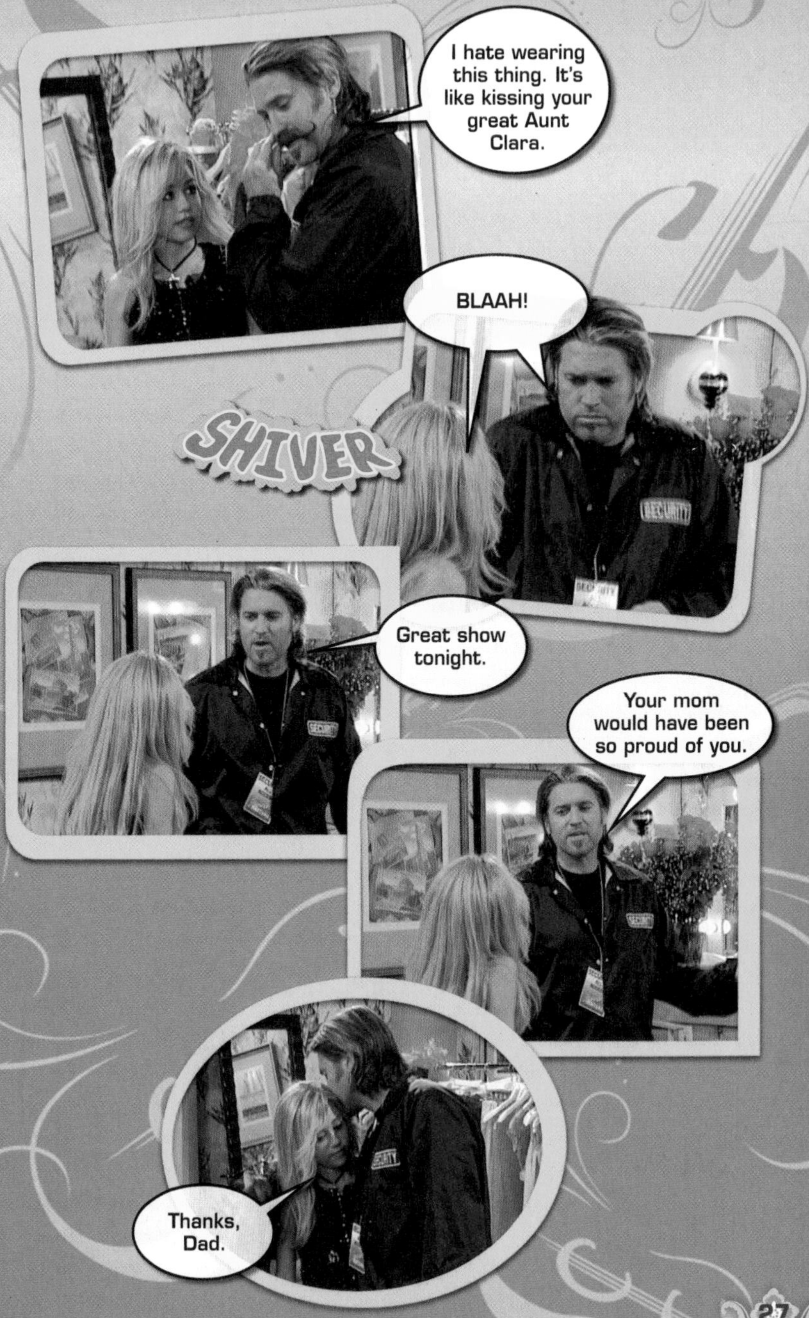
I hate wearing this thing. It's like kissing your great Aunt Clara.
BLAAH!
SHIVER
Great show tonight.
Your mom would have been so proud of you.
Thanks, Dad.

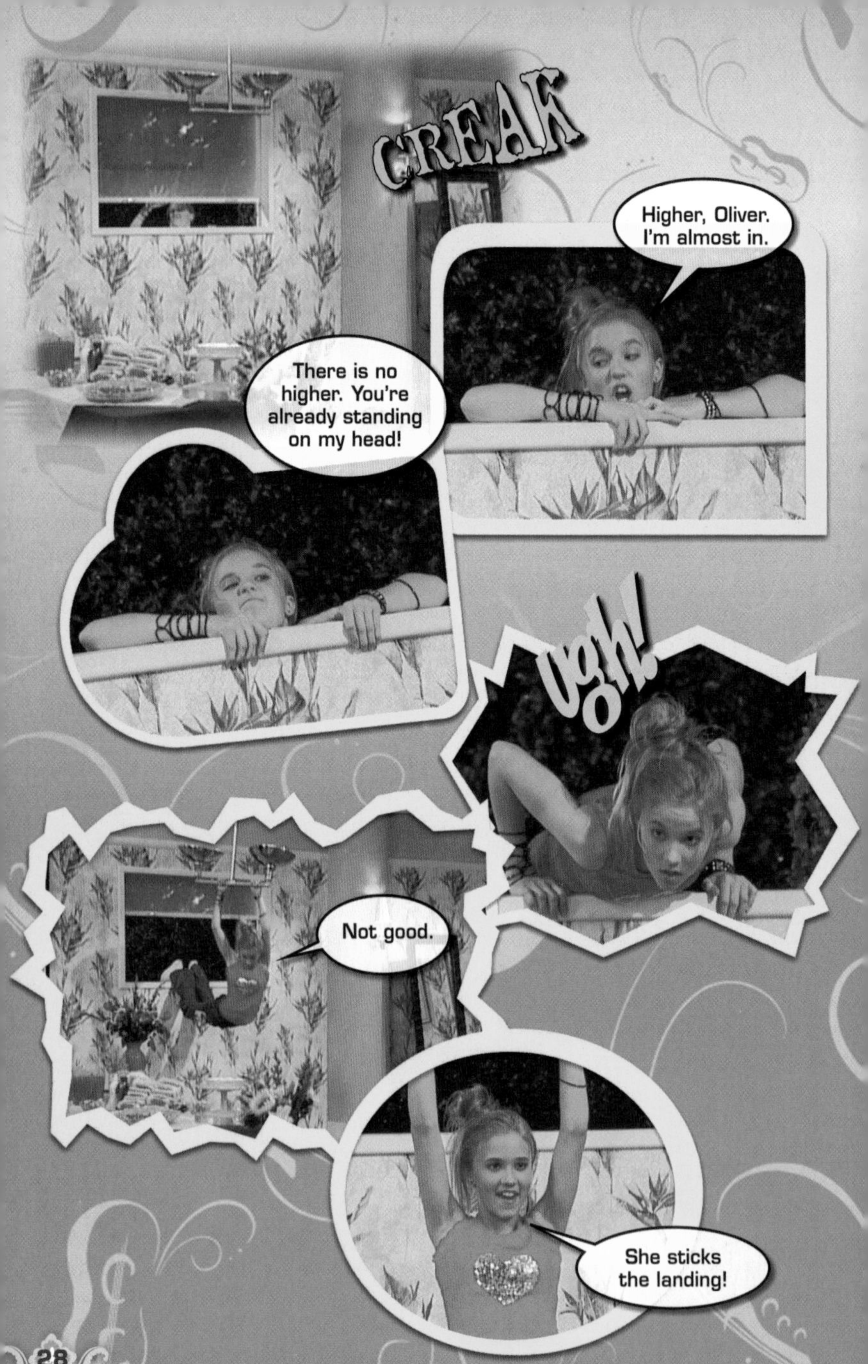
CREAK
Higher, Oliver. I'm almost in.
There is no higher. You're already standing on my head!
Ugh!
Not good.
She sticks the landing!

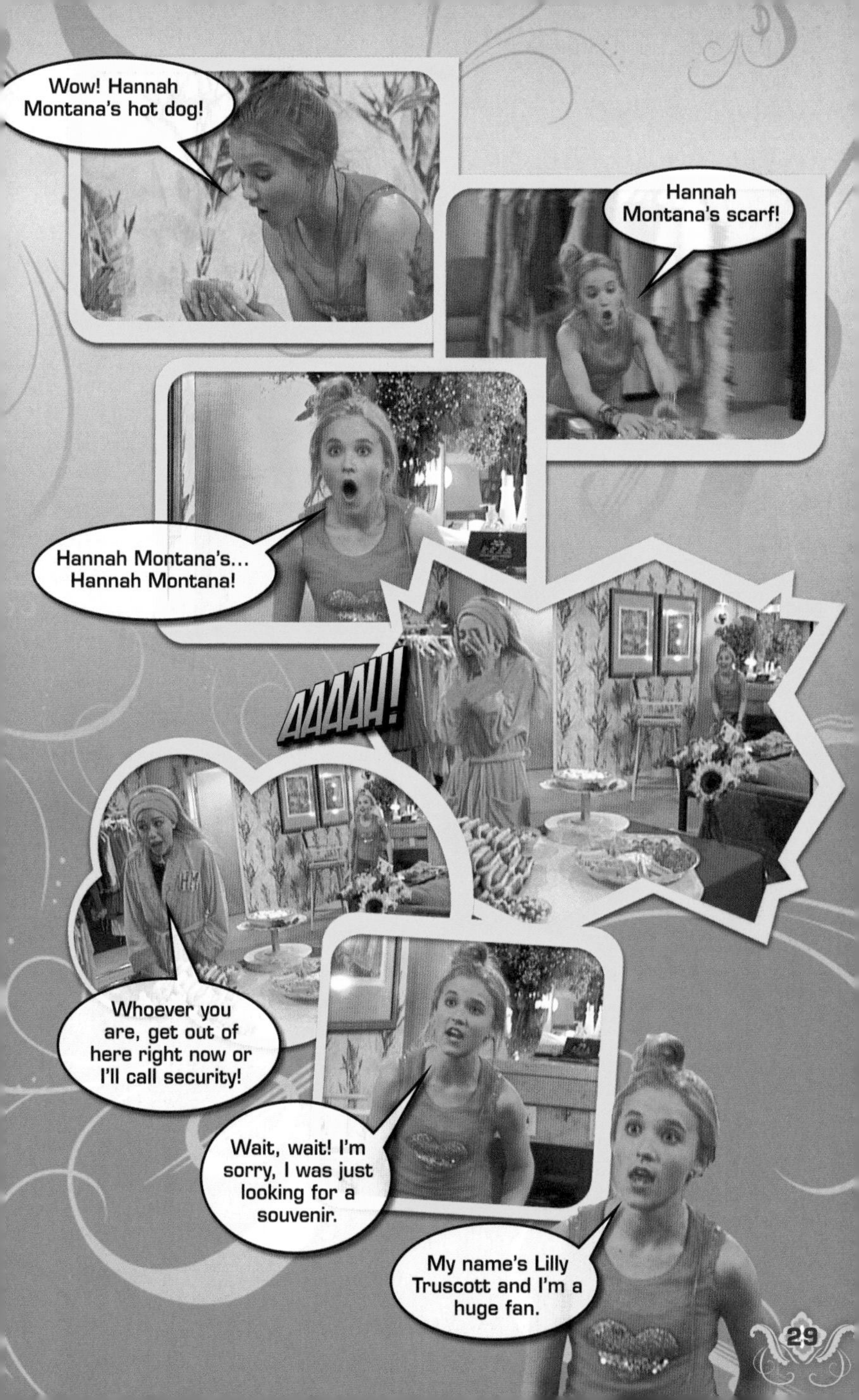
Wow! Hannah Montana's hot dog!
Hannah Montana's scarf!
Hannah Montana's... Hannah Montana!
AAAAH!
Whoever you are, get out of here right now or I'll call security!
Wait, wait! I'm sorry, I was just looking for a souvenir.
My name's Lilly Truscott and I'm a huge fan.

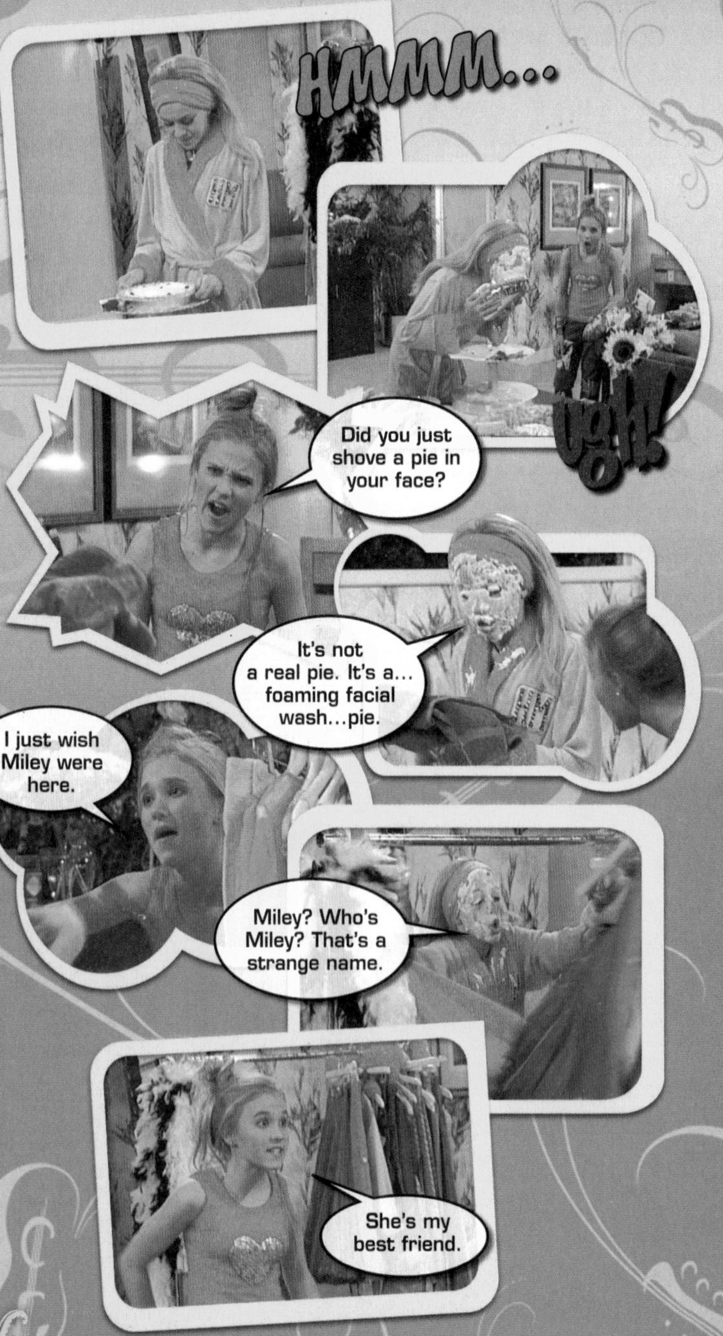
HMMM...
UGH!
Did you just shove a pie in your face?
It's not a real pie. It's a... foaming facial wash...pie.
I just wish Miley were here.
Miley? Who's Miley? That's a strange name.
She's my best friend.

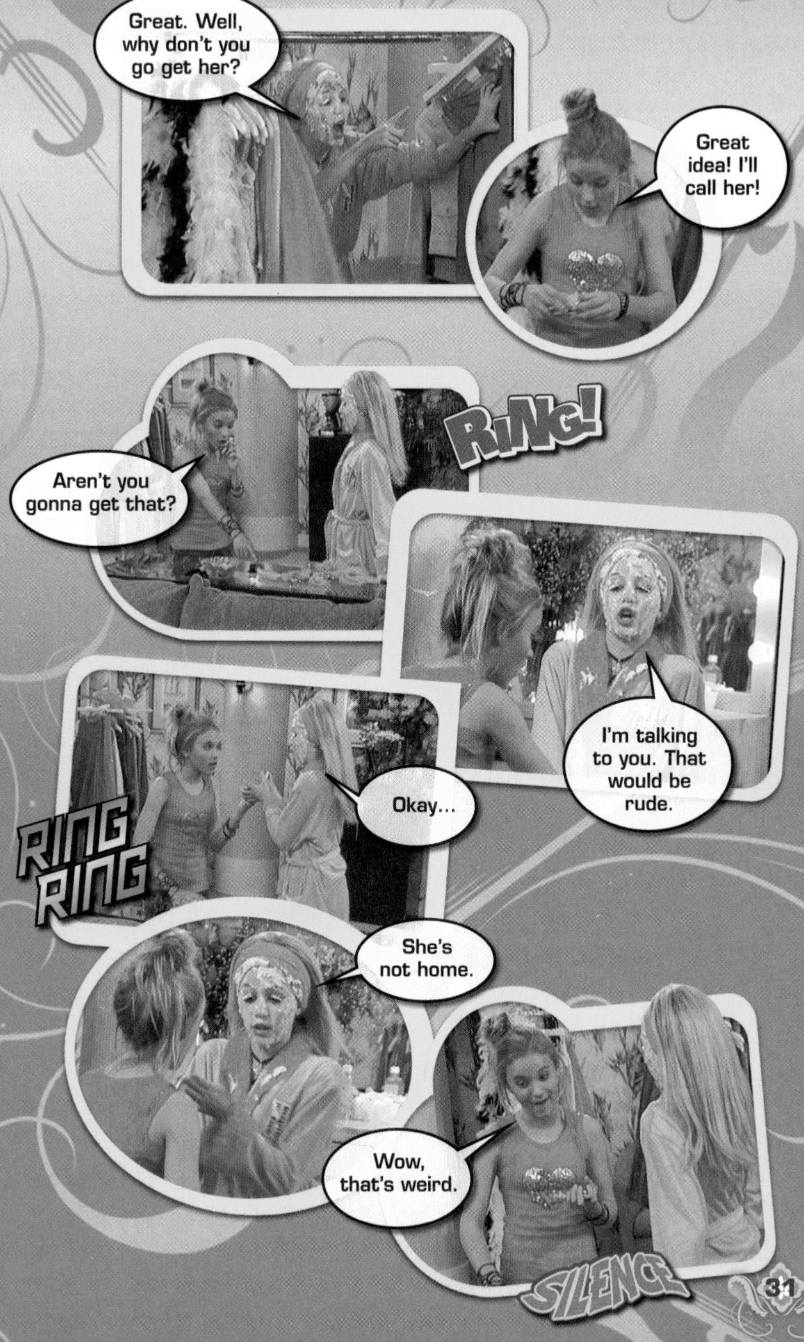
Great. Well, why don't you go get her?
Great idea! I'll call her!
RING!
Aren't you gonna get that?
I'm talking to you. That would be rude.
RING RING
Okay...
She's not home.
Wow, that's weird.
SILENCE

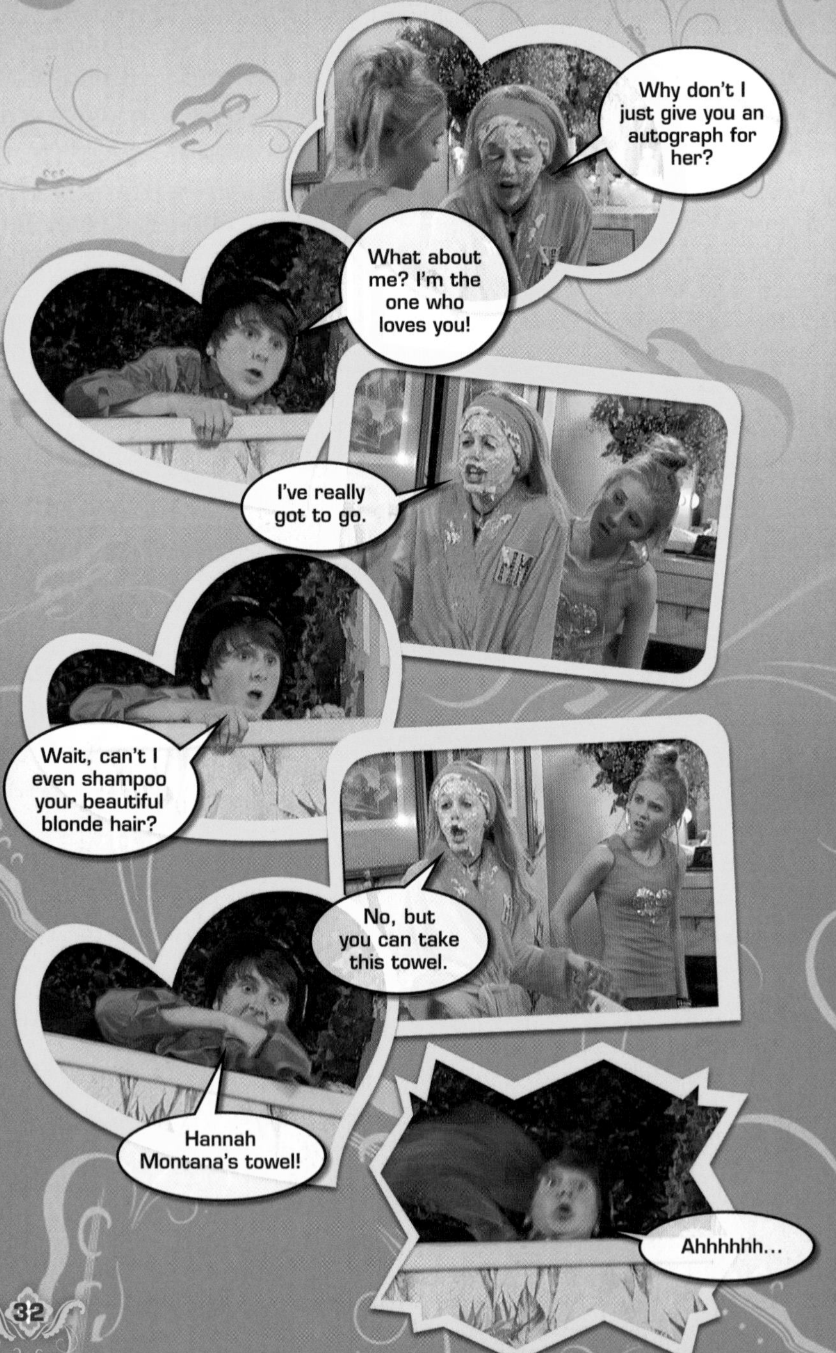
Why don't I just give you an autograph for her?
What about me? I'm the one who loves you!
I've really got to go.
Wait, can't I even shampoo your beautiful blonde hair?
No, but you can take this towel.
Hannah Montana's towel!
Ahhhhhh...

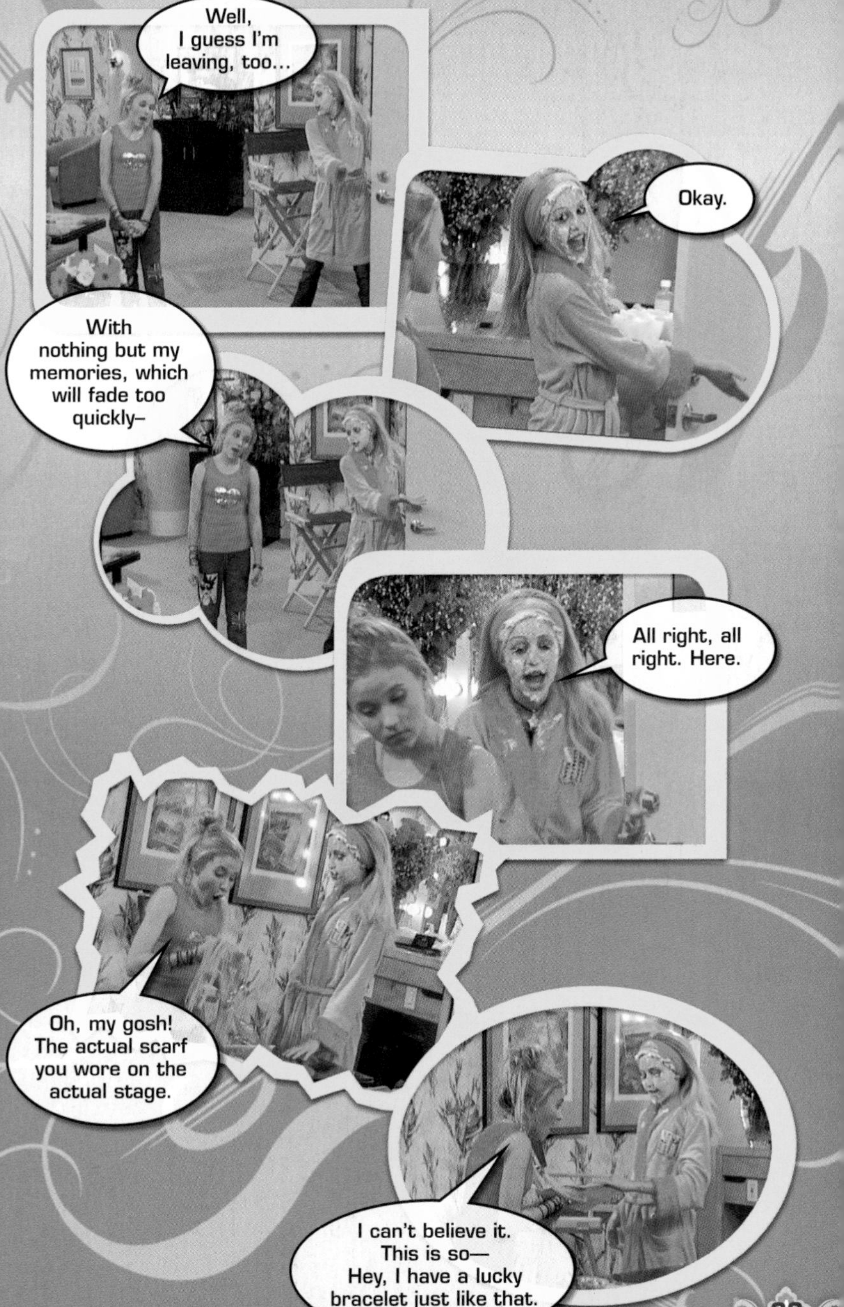
Well, I guess I'm leaving, too...
Okay.
With nothing but my memories, which will fade too quickly–
All right, all right. Here.
Oh, my gosh! The actual scarf you wore on the actual stage.
I can't believe it. This is so— Hey, I have a lucky bracelet just like that.

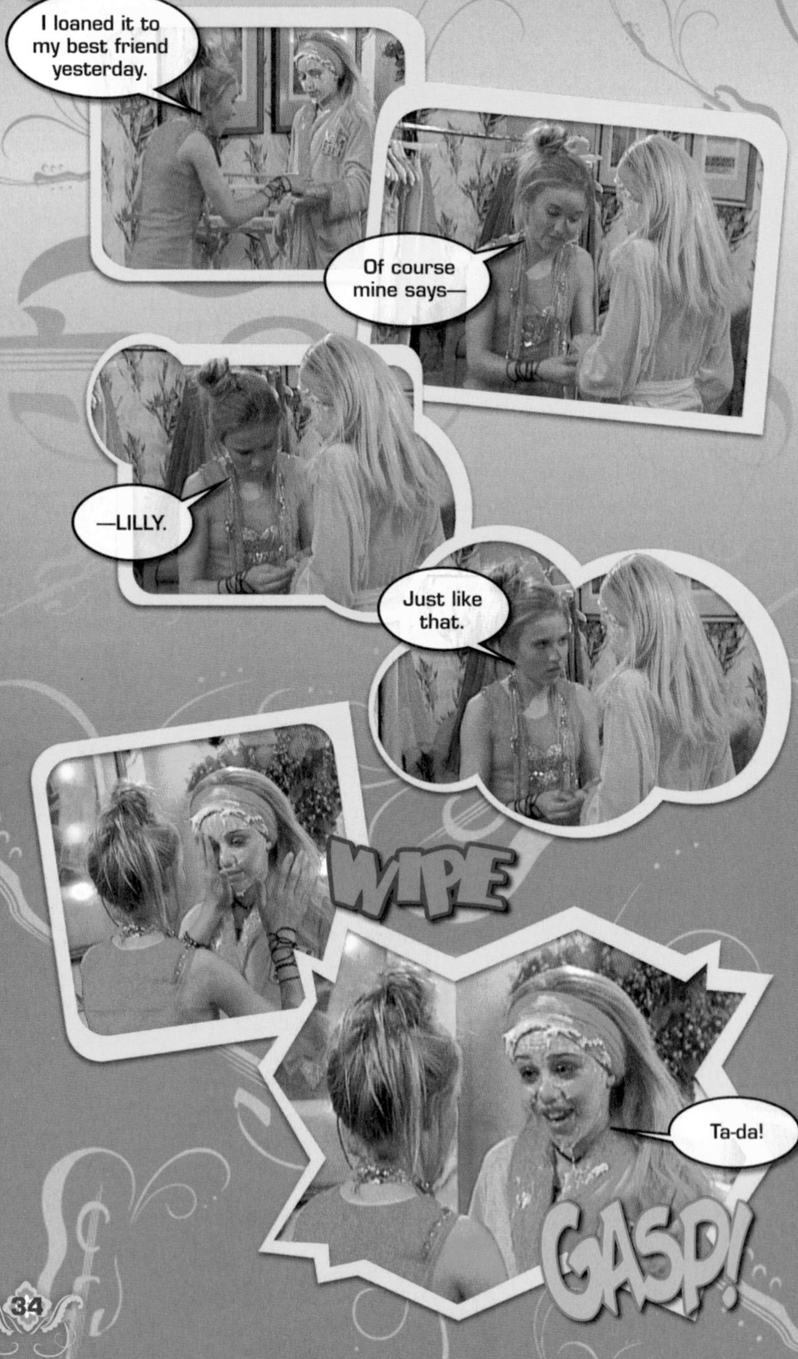
I loaned it to my best friend yesterday.
Of course mine says—
—LILLY.
Just like that.
WIPE
Ta-da!
GASP!

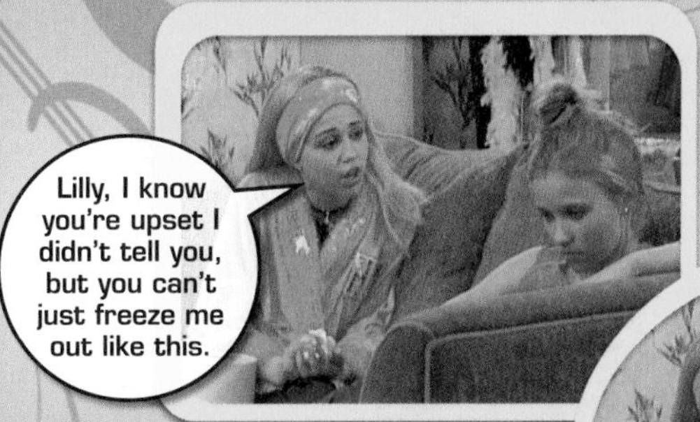
Lilly, I know you're upset I didn't tell you, but you can't just freeze me out like this.
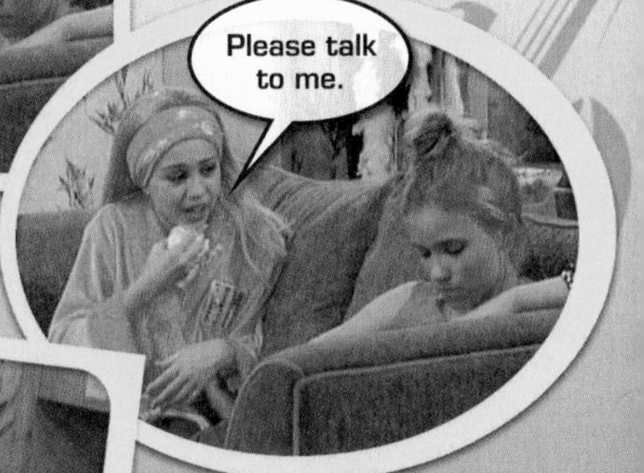
Please talk to me.
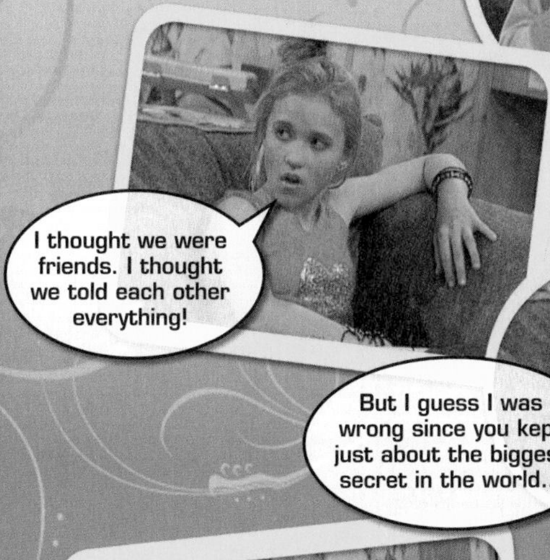
I thought we were friends. I thought we told each other everything!
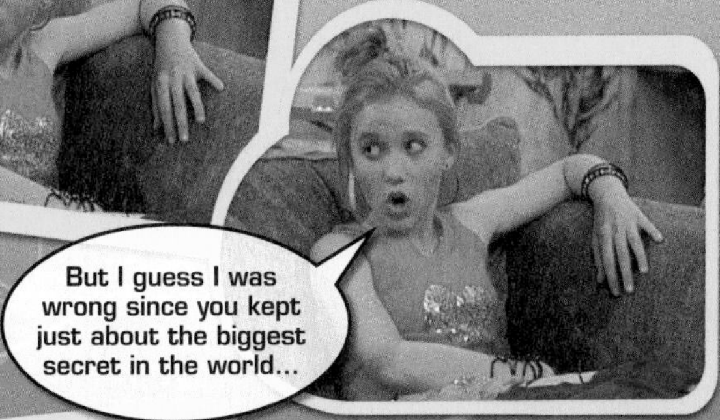
But I guess I was wrong since you kept just about the biggest secret in the world...
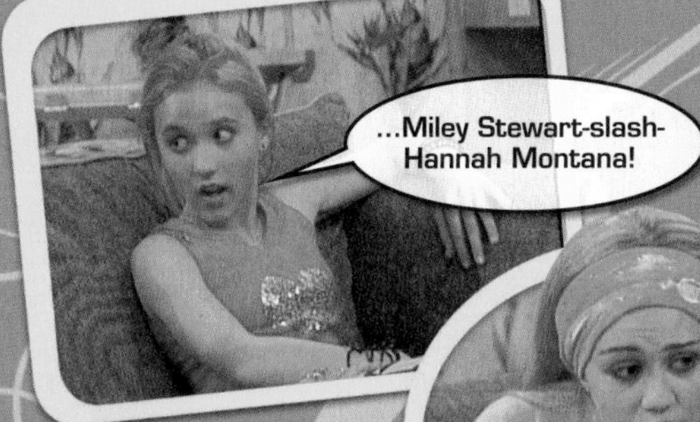
...Miley Stewart-slash-Hannah Montana!
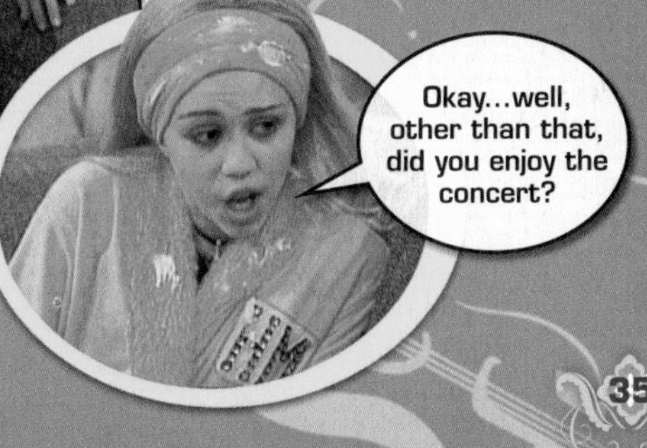
Okay...well, other than that, did you enjoy the concert?

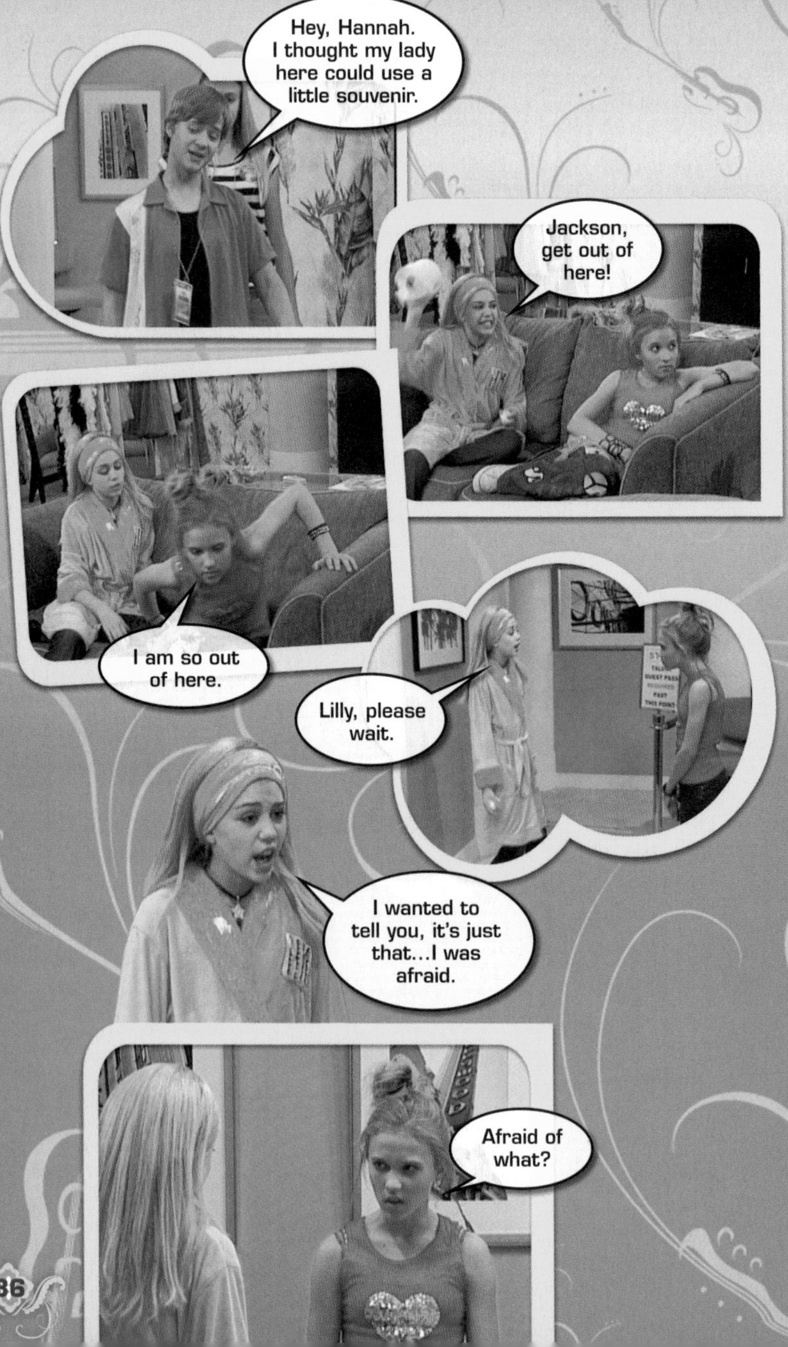
Hey, Hannah. I thought my lady here could use a little souvenir.
Jackson, get out of here!
I am so out of here.
Lilly, please wait.
I wanted to tell you, it's just that...I was afraid.
Afraid of what?

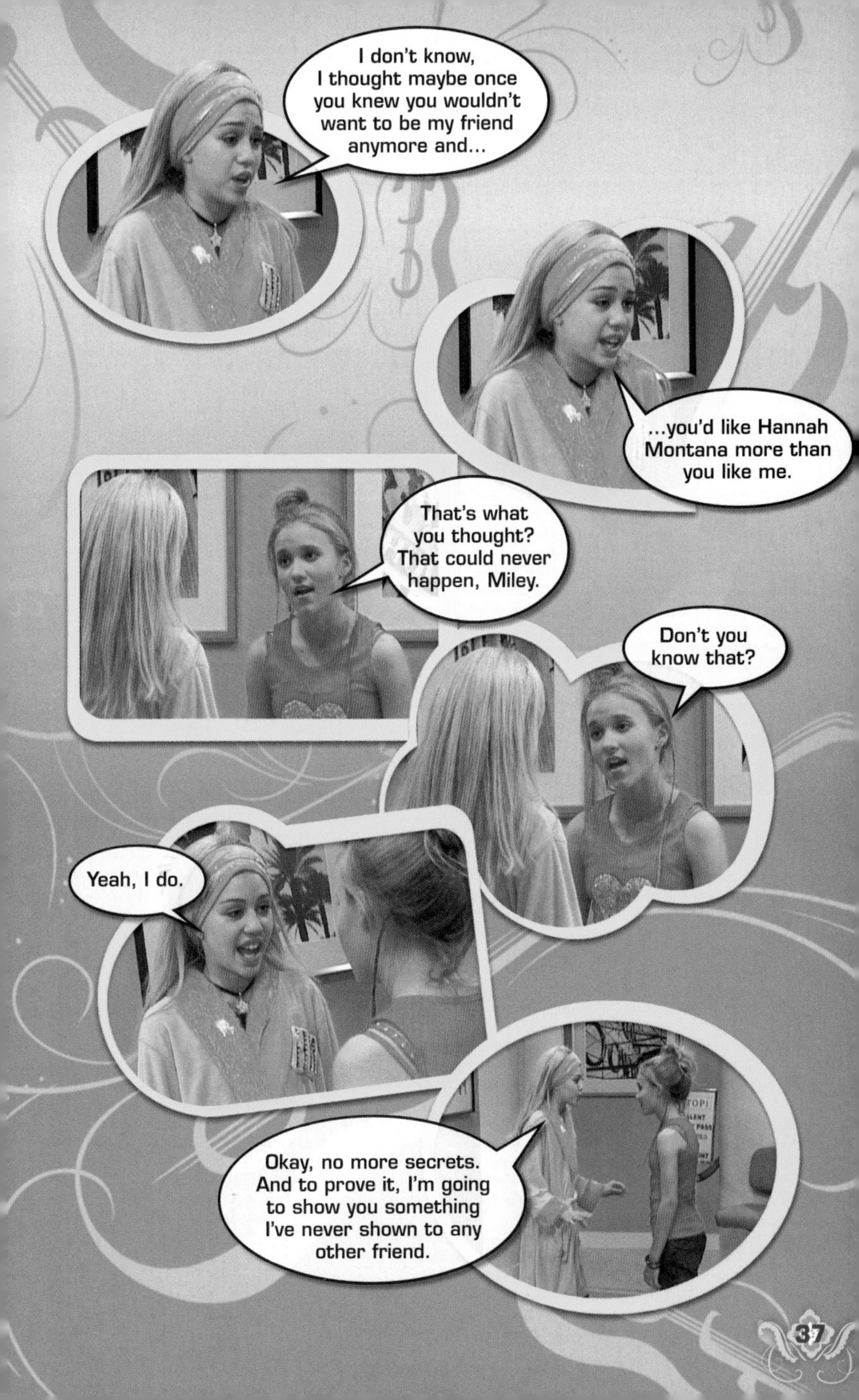
I don't know, I thought maybe once you knew you wouldn't want to be my friend anymore and...
...you'd like Hannah Montana more than you like me.
That's what you thought? That could never happen, Miley.
Don't you know that?
Yeah, I do.
Okay, no more secrets. And to prove it, I'm going to show you something I've never shown to any other friend.

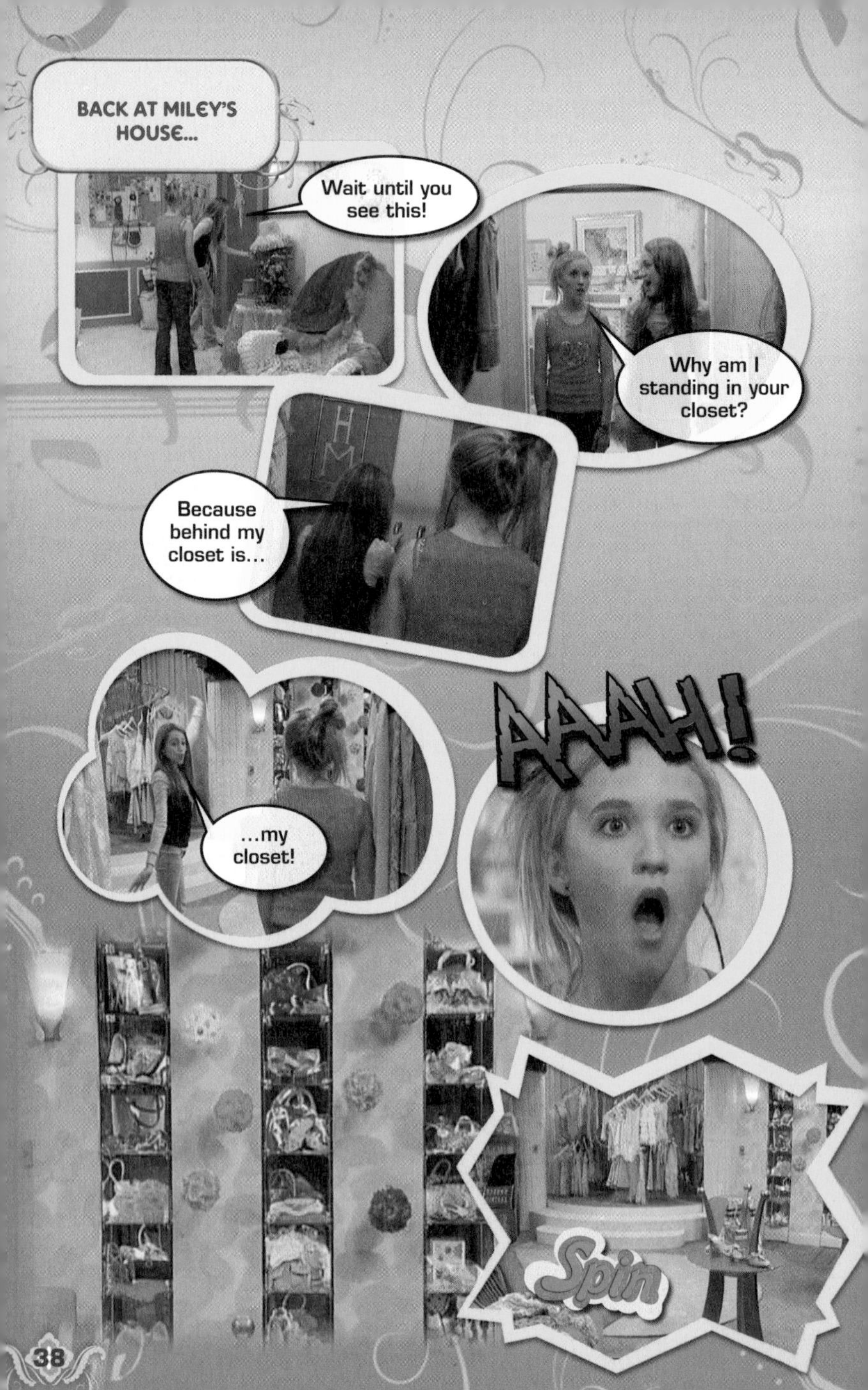
BACK AT MILEY'S HOUSE...
Wait until you see this!
Why am I standing in your closet?
Because behind my closet is...
...my closet!
AAAH!
Spin

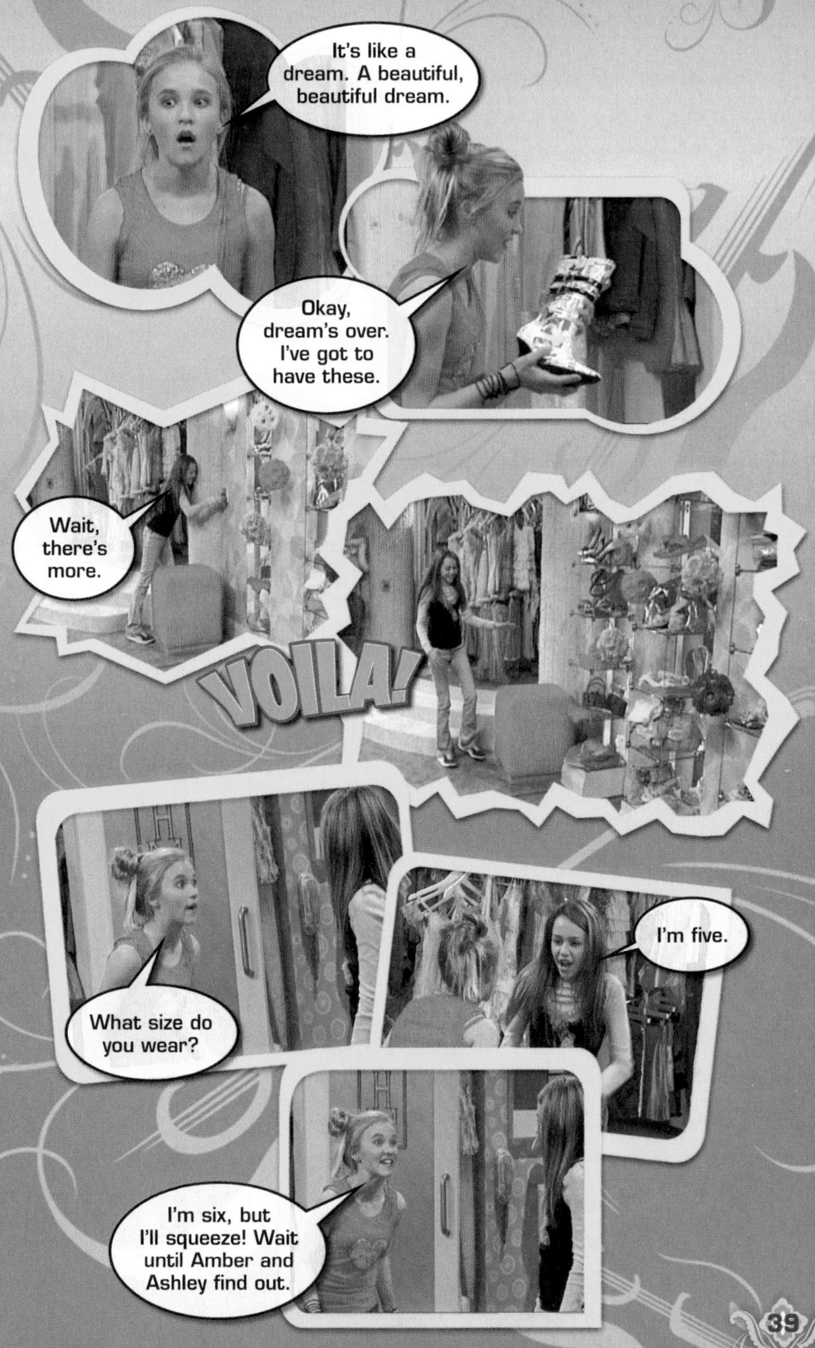
It's like a dream. A beautiful, beautiful dream.
Okay, dream's over. I've got to have these.
Wait, there's more.
VOILA!
What size do you wear?
I'm five.
I'm six, but I'll squeeze! Wait until Amber and Ashley find out.

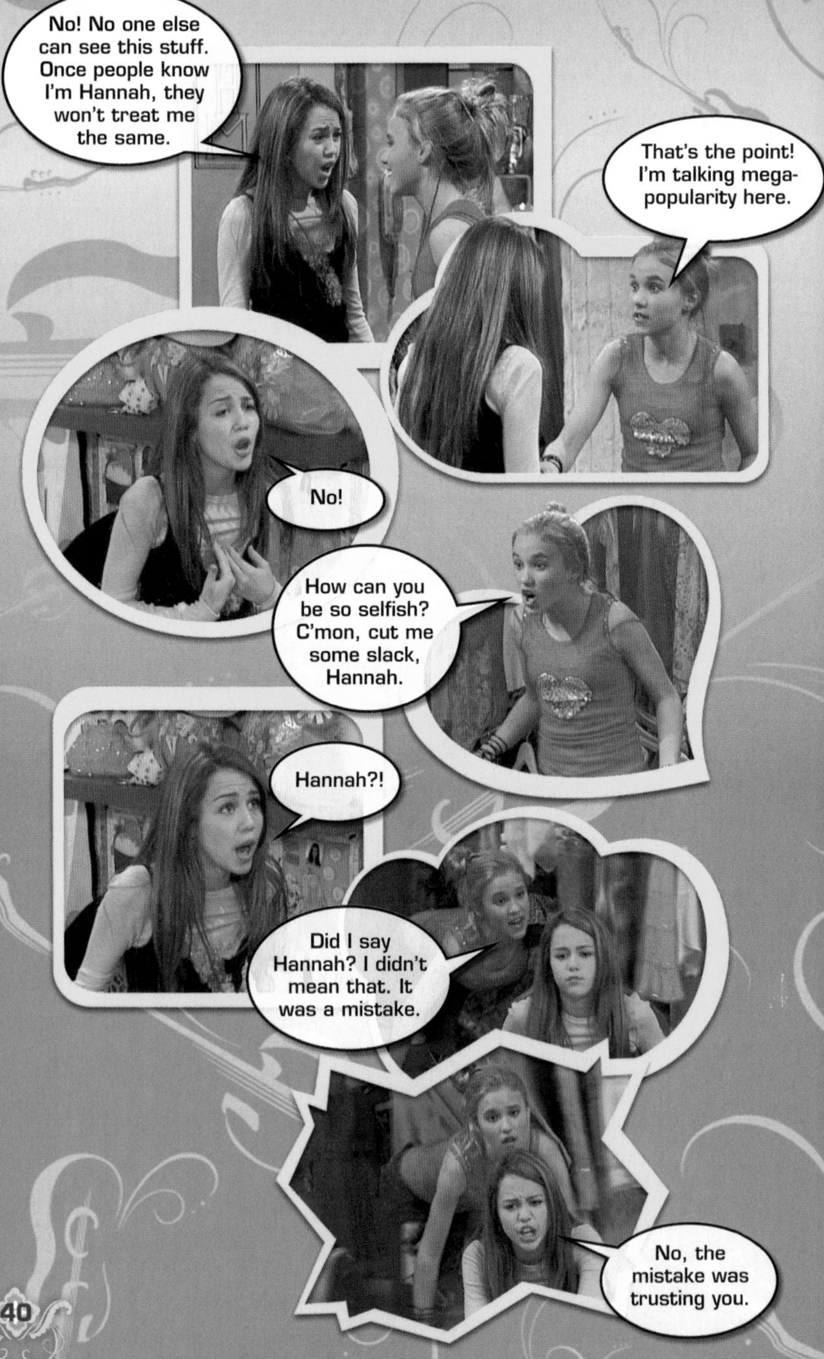
No! No one else can see this stuff. Once people know I'm Hannah, they won't treat me the same.
That's the point! I'm talking mega-popularity here.
No!
How can you be so selfish? C'mon, cut me some slack, Hannah.
Hannah?!
Did I say Hannah? I didn't mean that. It was a mistake.
No, the mistake was trusting you.

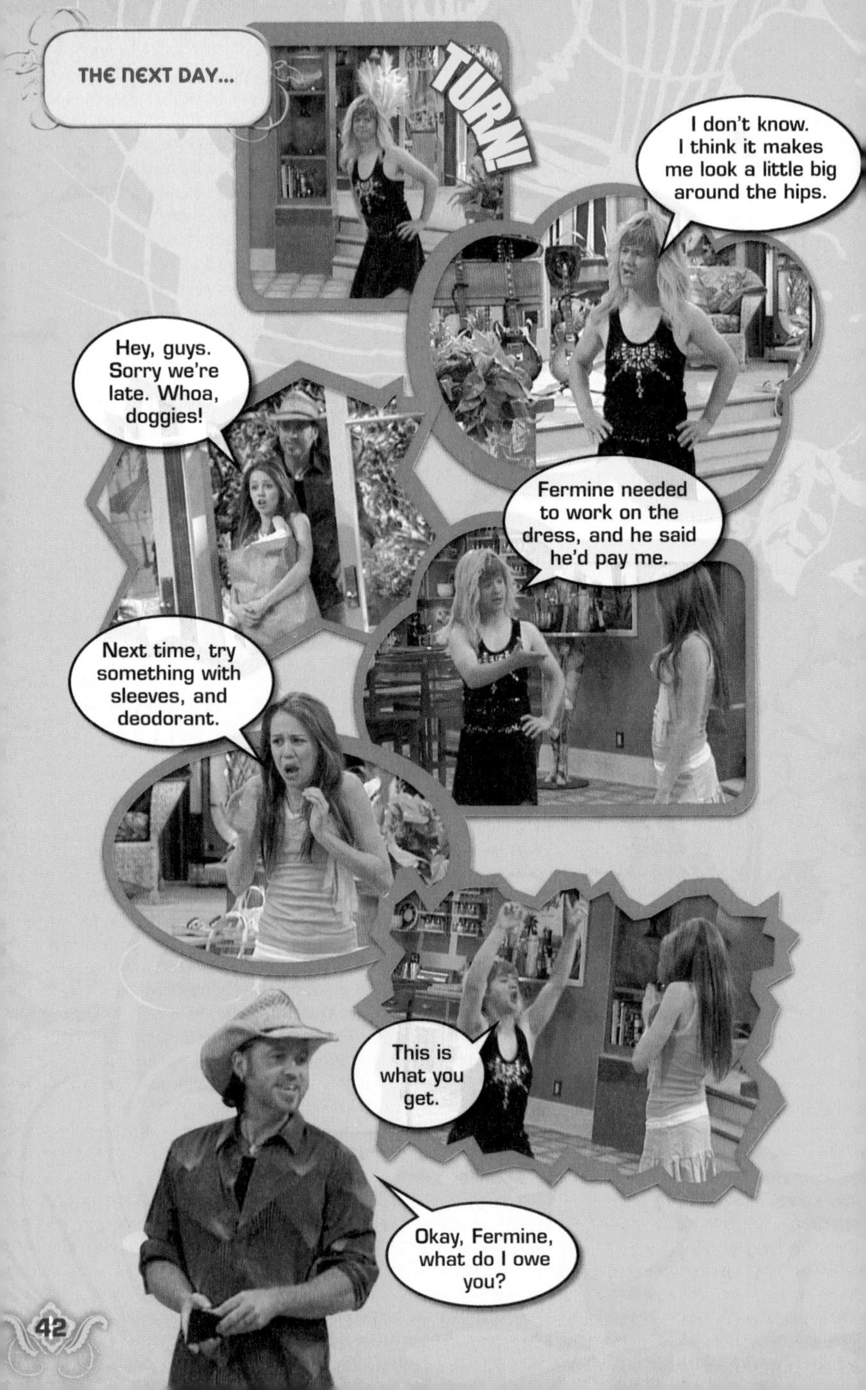
THE NEXT DAY...
TURN!
I don't know. I think it makes me look a little big around the hips.
Hey, guys. Sorry we're late. Whoa, doggies!
Fermine needed to work on the dress, and he said he'd pay me.
Next time, try something with sleeves, and deodorant.
This is what you get.
Okay, Fermine, what do I owe you?

43

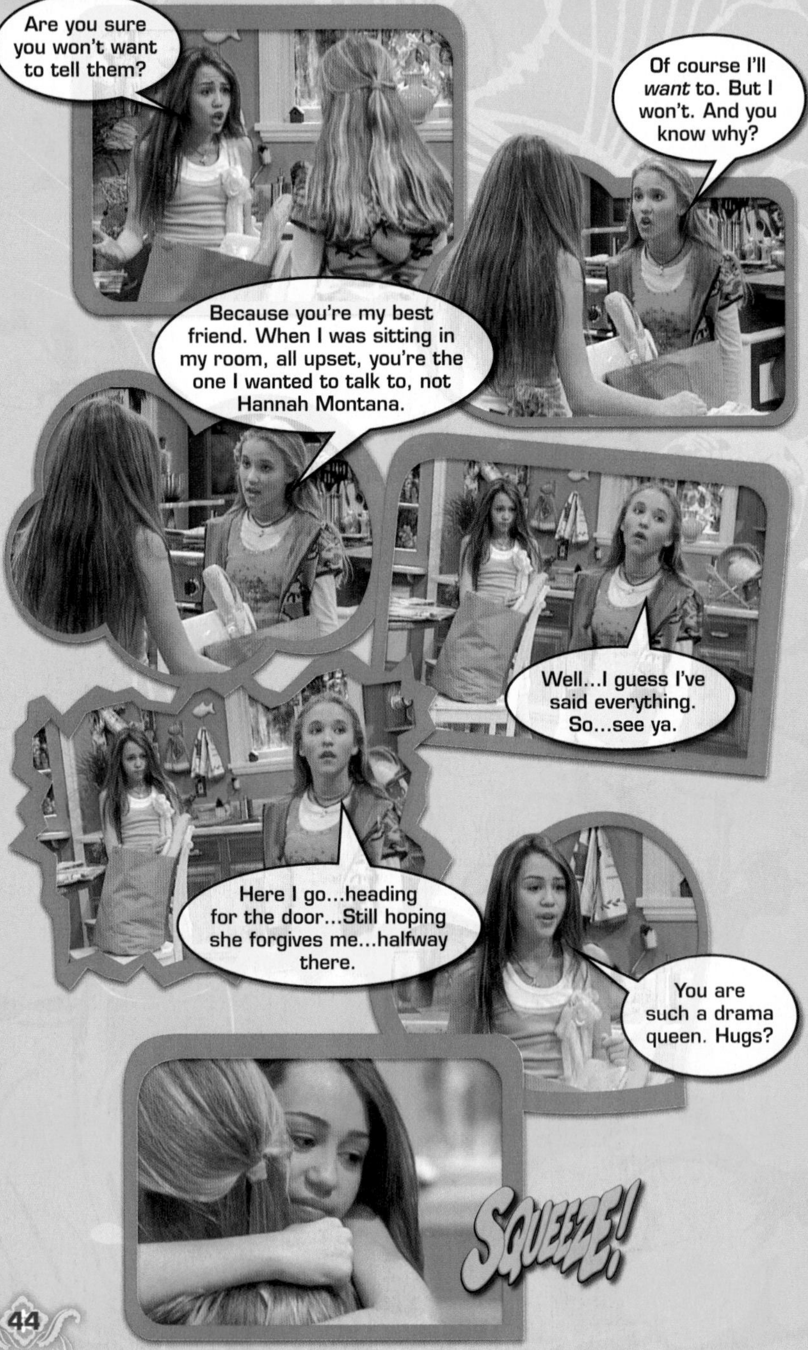

Are you sure you won't want to tell them?
Of course I'll *want* to. But I won't. And you know why?
Because you're my best friend. When I was sitting in my room, all upset, you're the one I wanted to talk to, not Hannah Montana.
Well...I guess I've said everything. So...see ya.
Here I go...heading for the door...Still hoping she forgives me...halfway there.
You are such a drama queen. Hugs?
SQUEEZE!

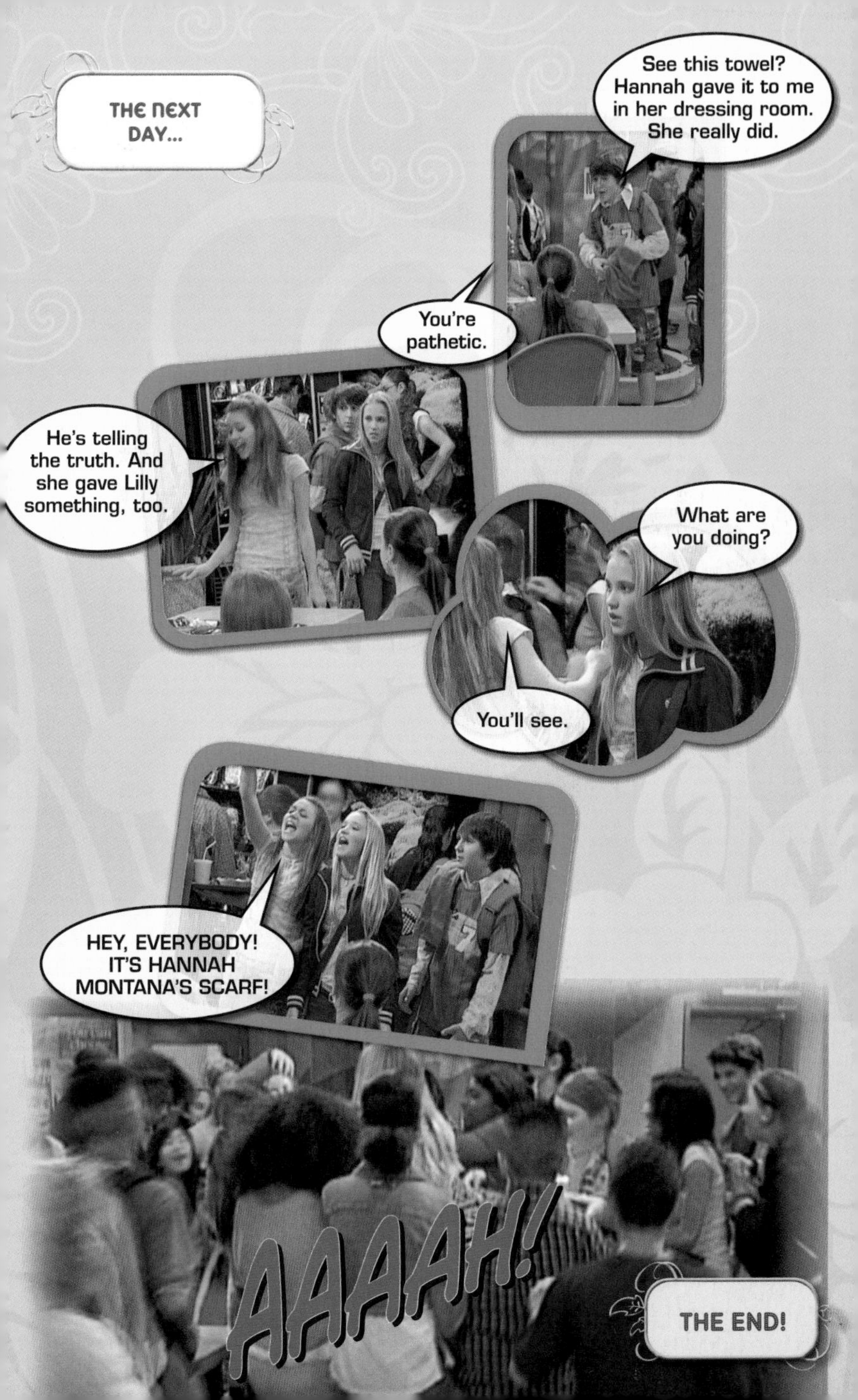
THE NEXT DAY...
See this towel? Hannah gave it to me in her dressing room. She really did.
You're pathetic.
He's telling the truth. And she gave Lilly something, too.
What are you doing?
You'll see.
HEY, EVERYBODY! IT'S HANNAH MONTANA'S SCARF!
AAAAH!
THE END!

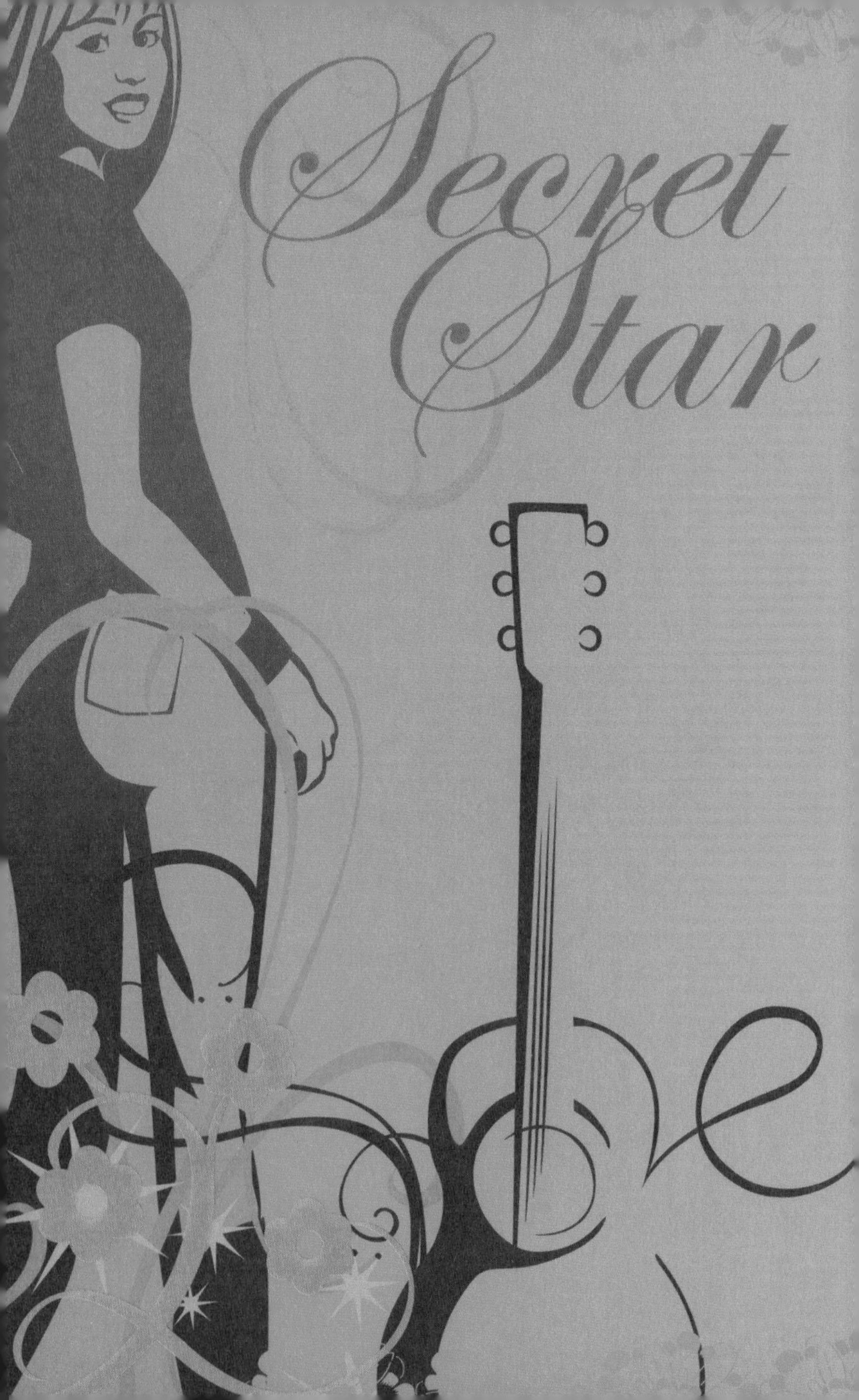
Secret Star

"SHE'S A SUPER SNEAK"

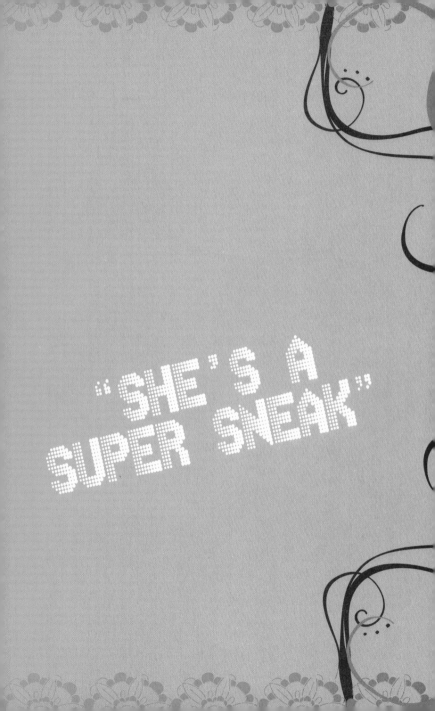

48

49

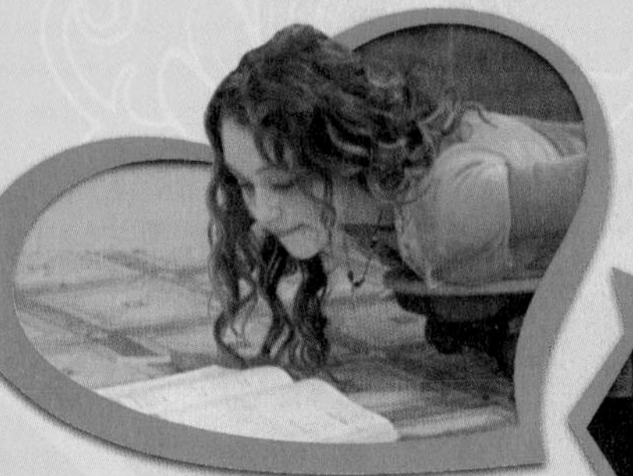

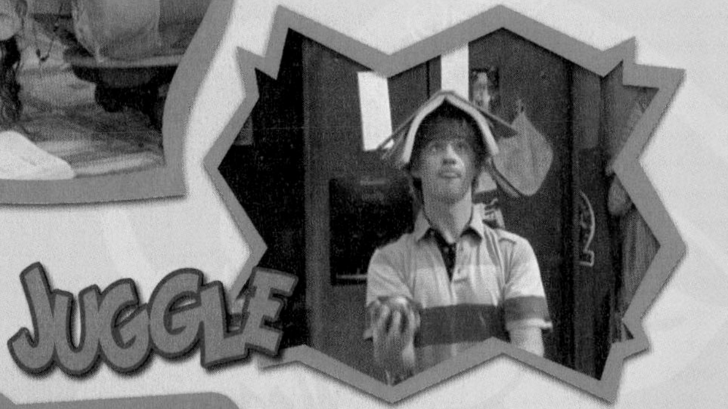
JUGGLE

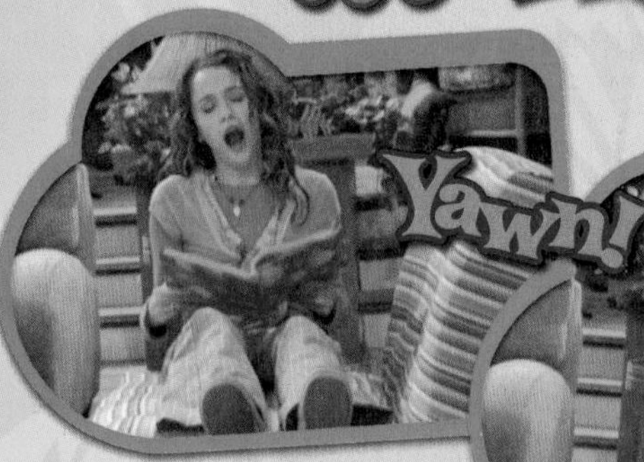
Yawn!

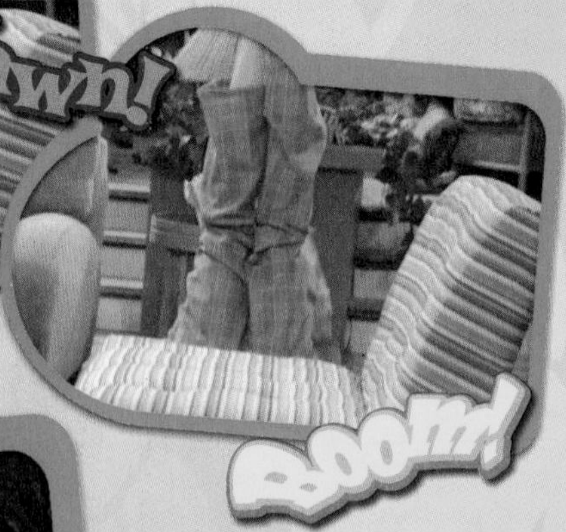
Boom!

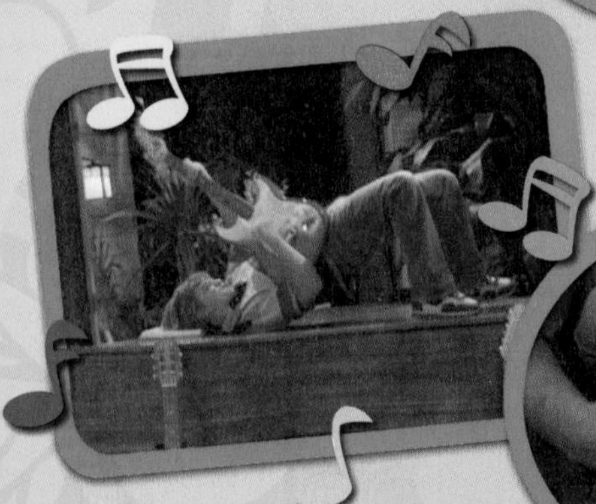

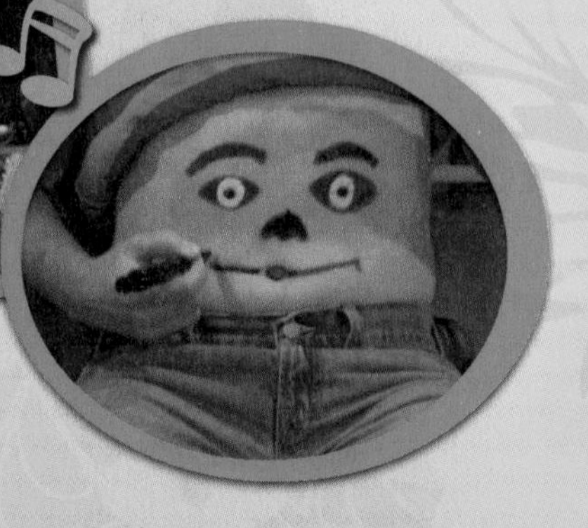

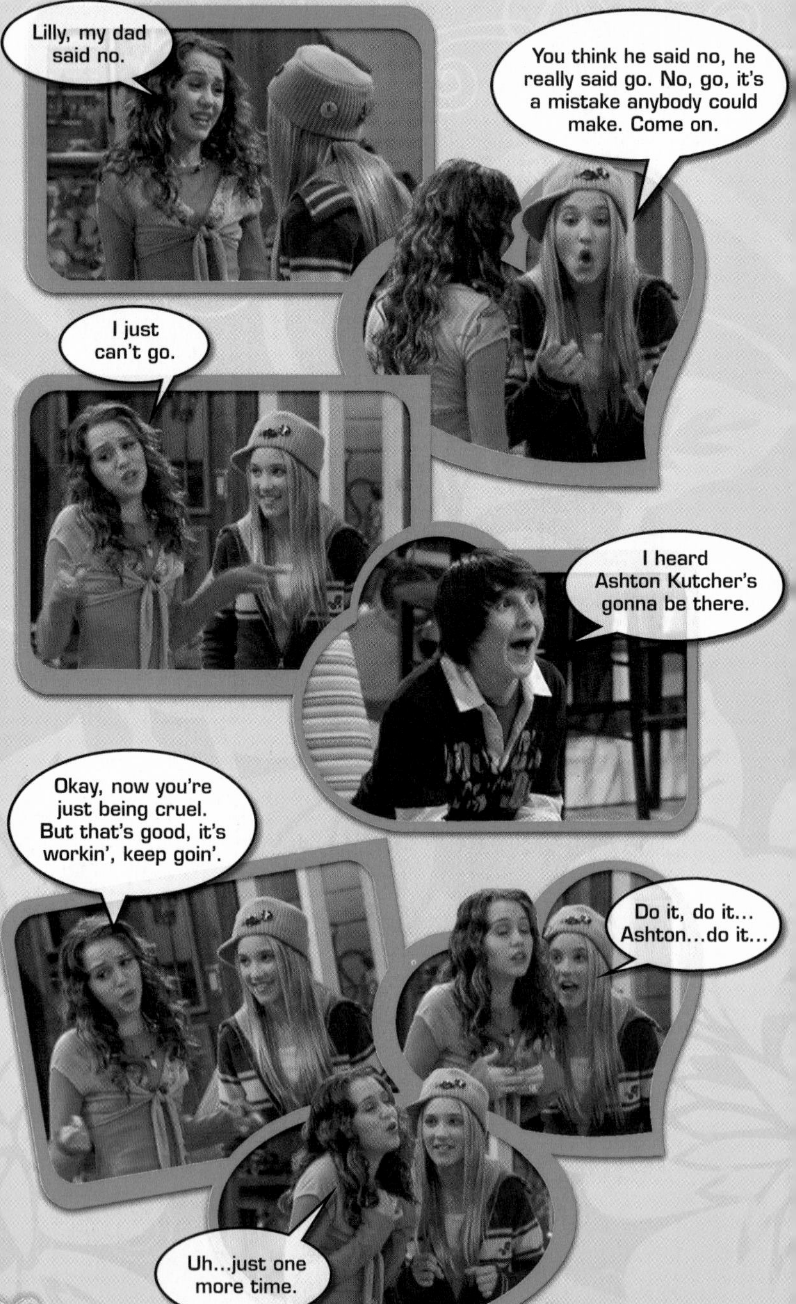
Lilly, my dad said no.
You think he said no, he really said go. No, go, it's a mistake anybody could make. Come on.
I just can't go.
I heard Ashton Kutcher's gonna be there.
Okay, now you're just being cruel. But that's good, it's workin', keep goin'.
Do it, do it... Ashton...do it...
Uh...just one more time.

whisper

57

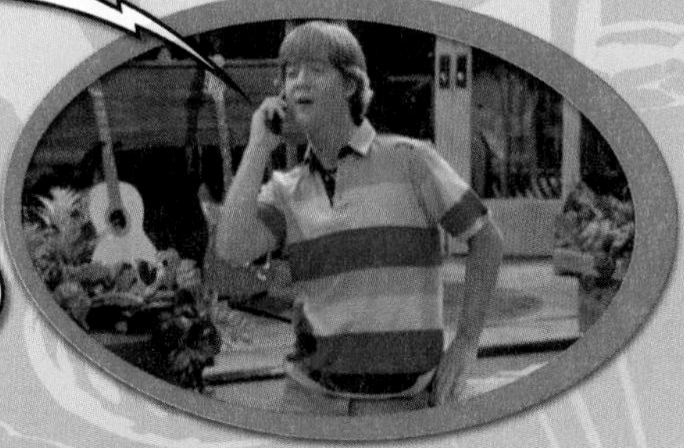
Theater three? I'm guessing it's very close to theater two. Can't you see I'm on the phone?
I swear, people get dumber and dumber every day.

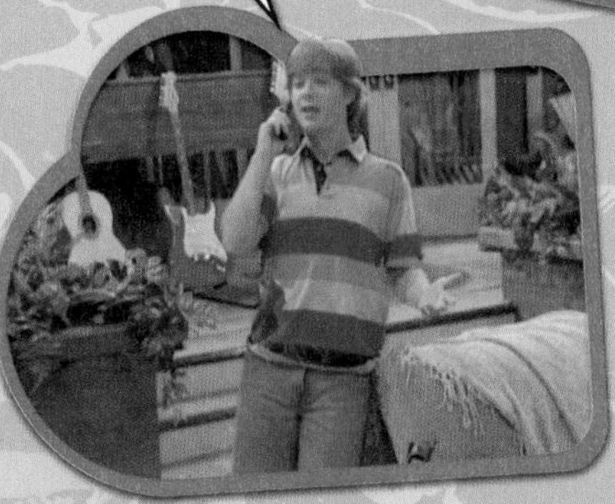
Hello! You're costing me minutes here!

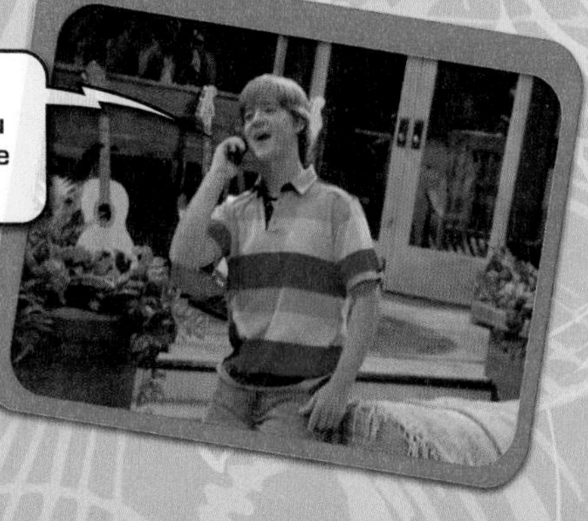
And I'm telling you this on the D.L.

60

61

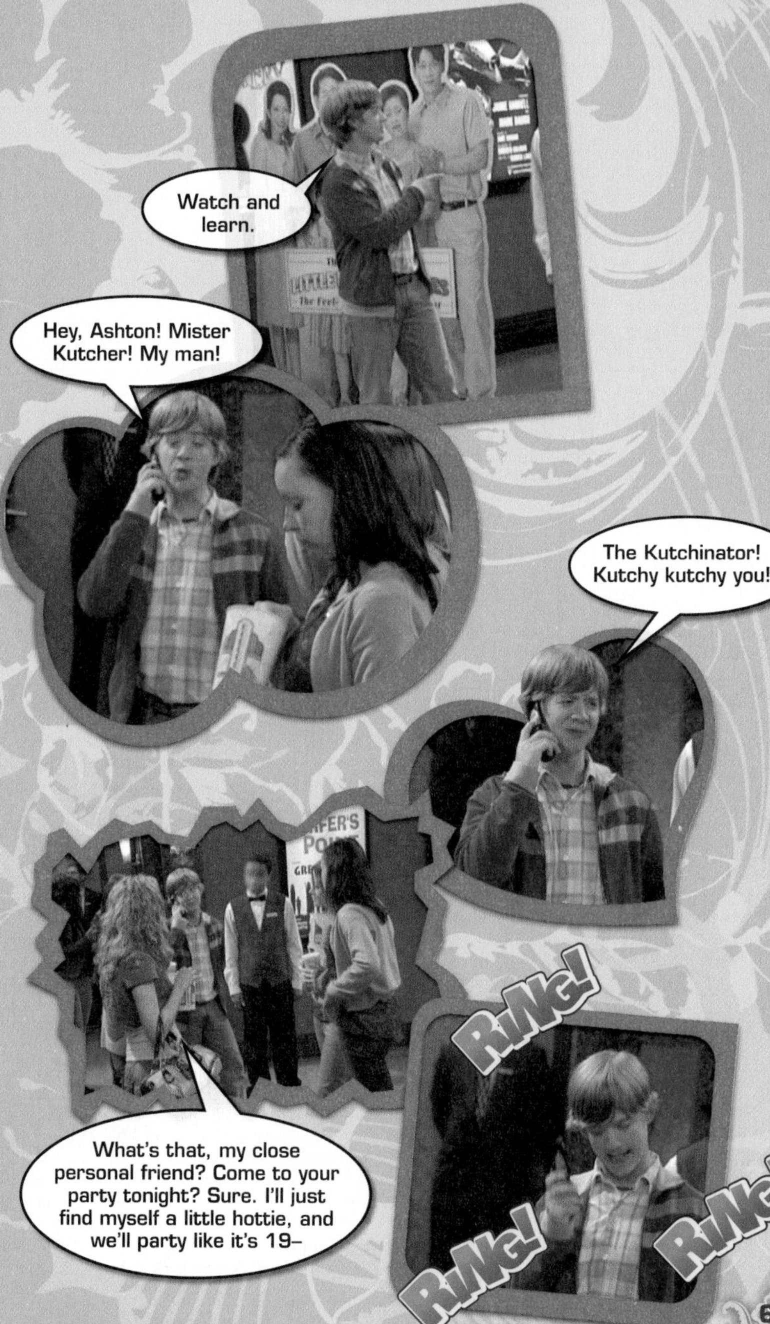

Watch and learn.
Hey, Ashton! Mister Kutcher! My man!
The Kutchinator! Kutchy kutchy you!
What's that, my close personal friend? Come to your party tonight? Sure. I'll just find myself a little hottie, and we'll party like it's 19–
RiNG!
RiNG!
RiNG!

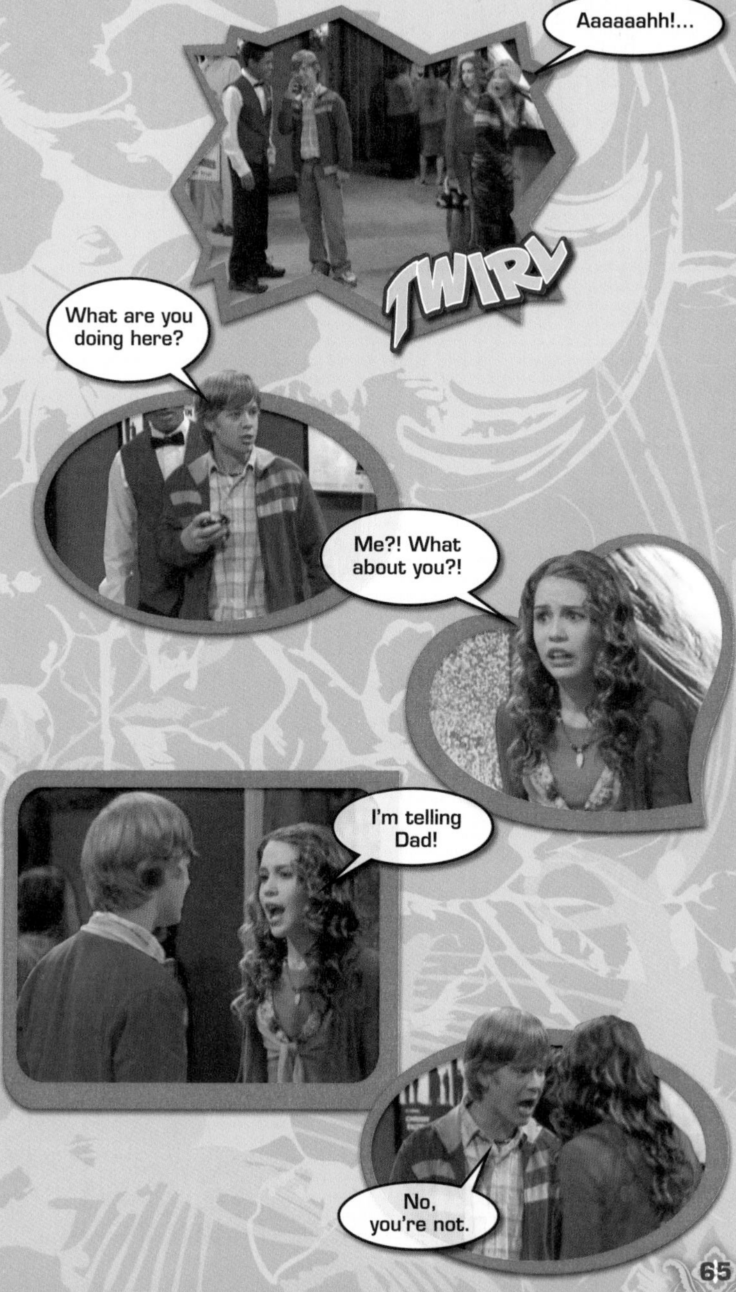
Aaaaaahh!...
TWIRL
What are you doing here?
Me?! What about you?!
I'm telling Dad!
No, you're not.

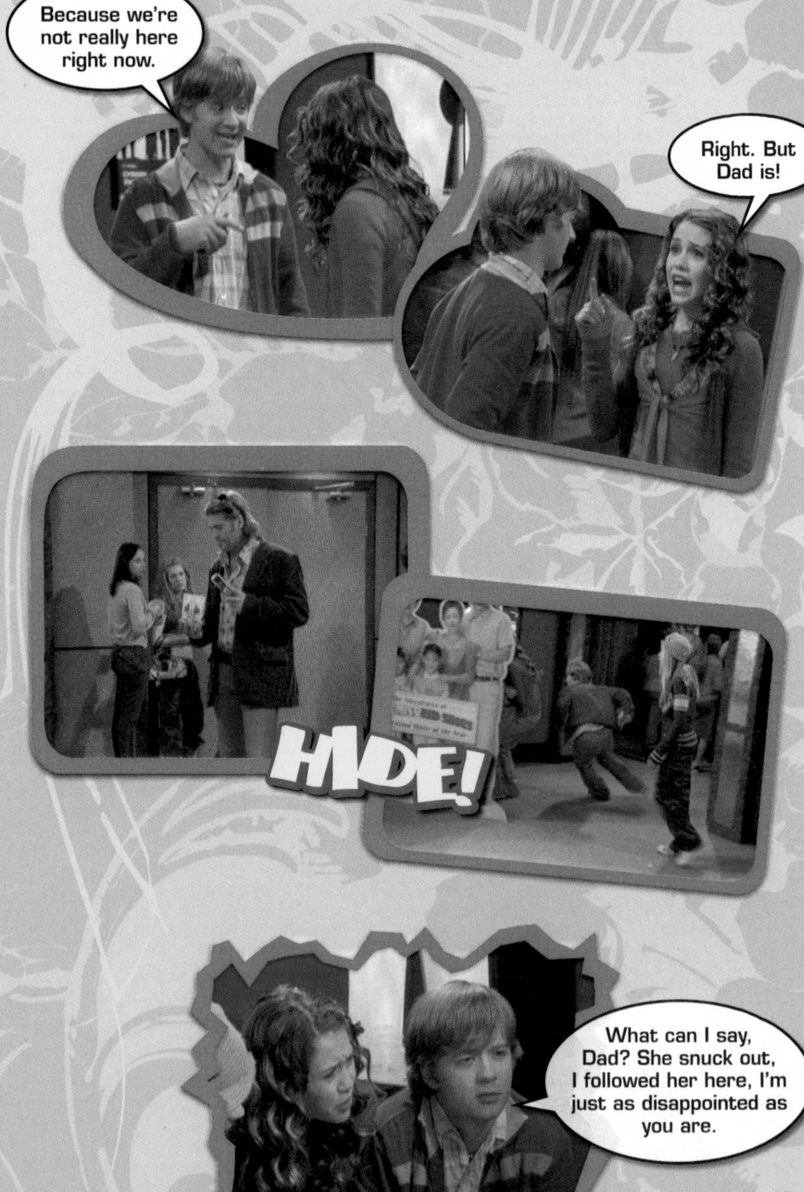
Because we're not really here right now.
Right. But Dad is!
HIDE!
What can I say, Dad? She snuck out, I followed her here, I'm just as disappointed as you are.

67

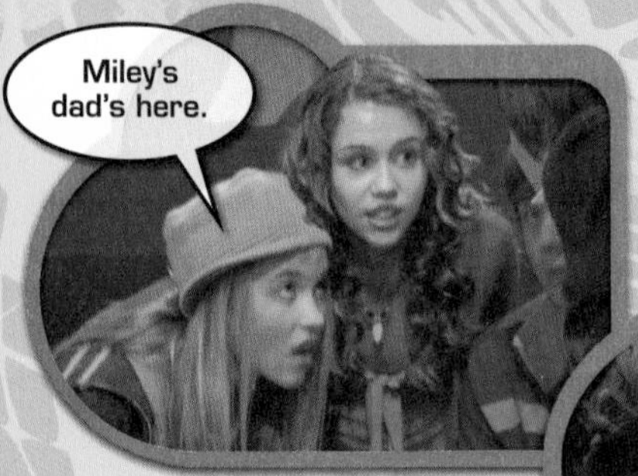
Miley's dad's here.

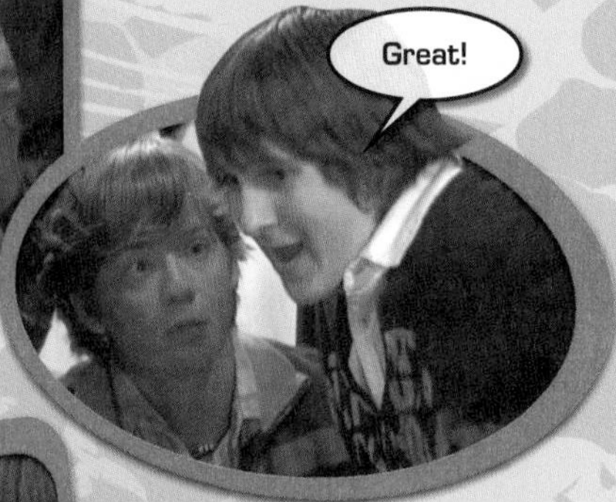
Great!

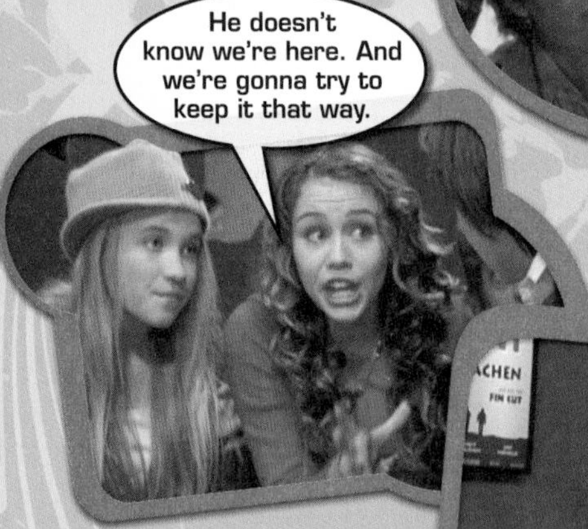
He doesn't know we're here. And we're gonna try to keep it that way.

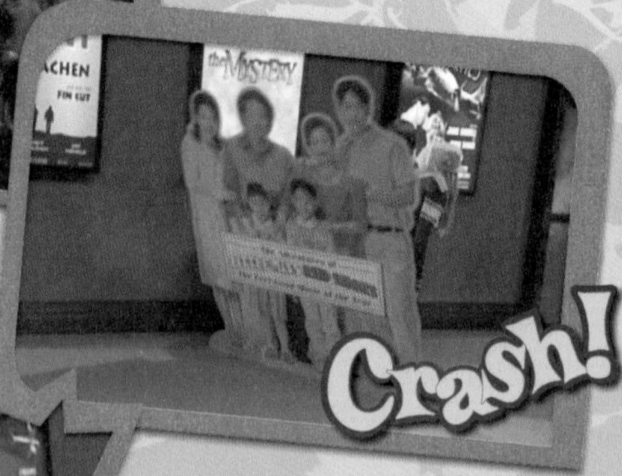
Crash!

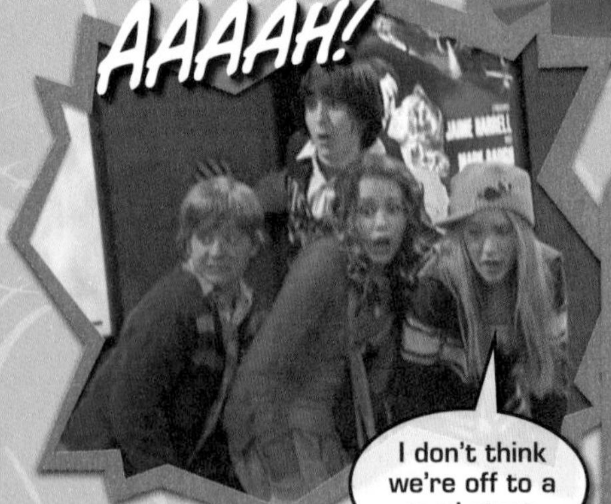
AAAAH!
I don't think we're off to a good start.

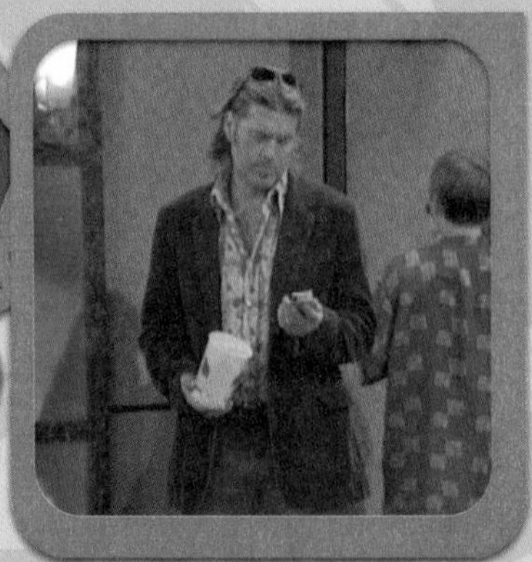

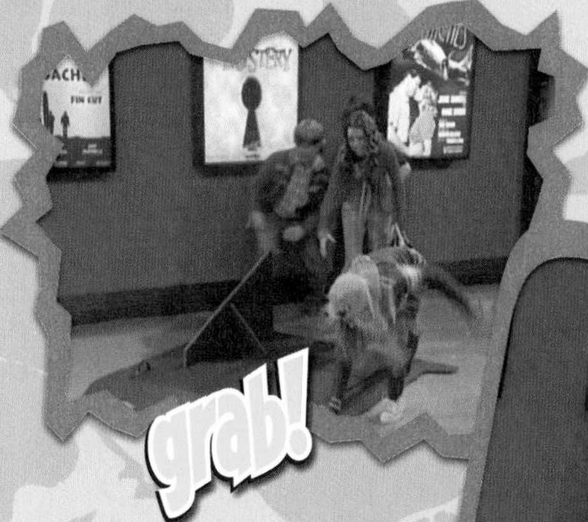
grab!

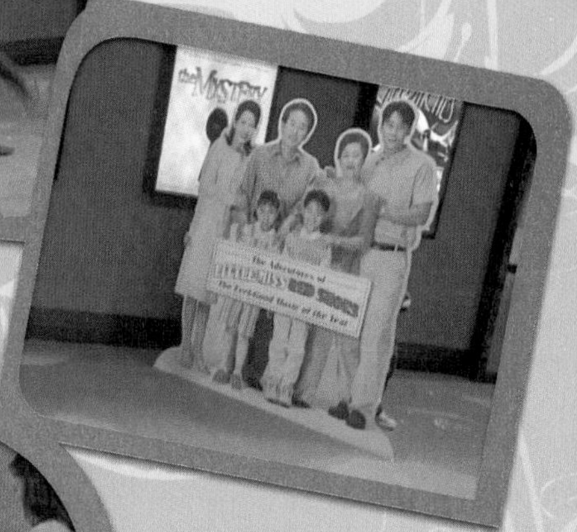

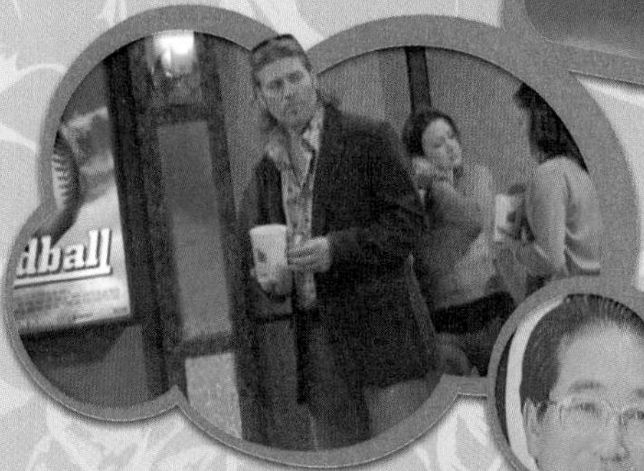

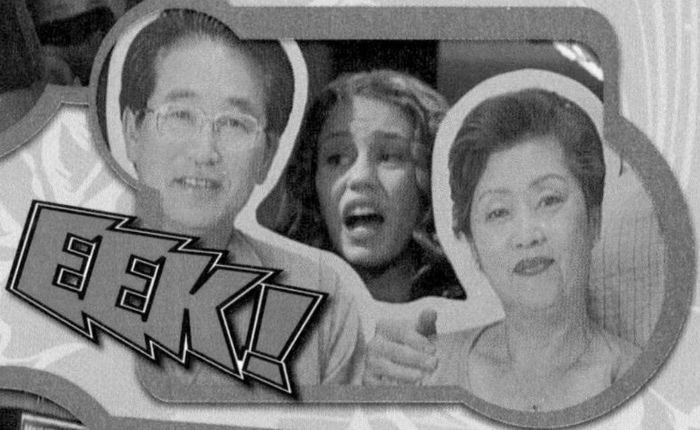
EEK!

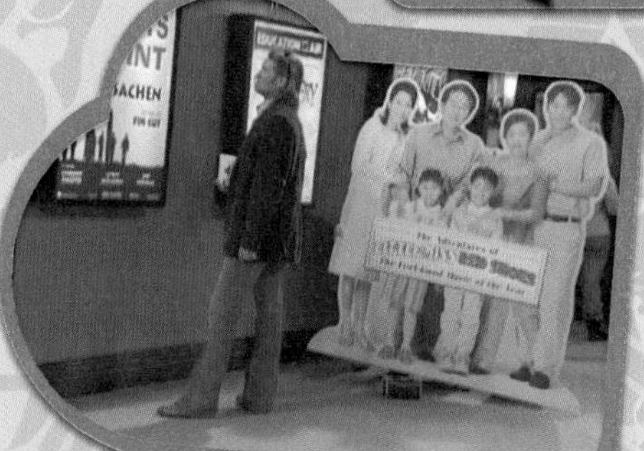

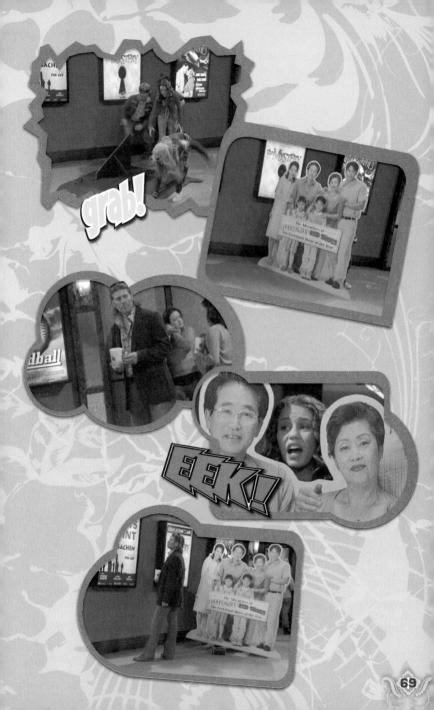

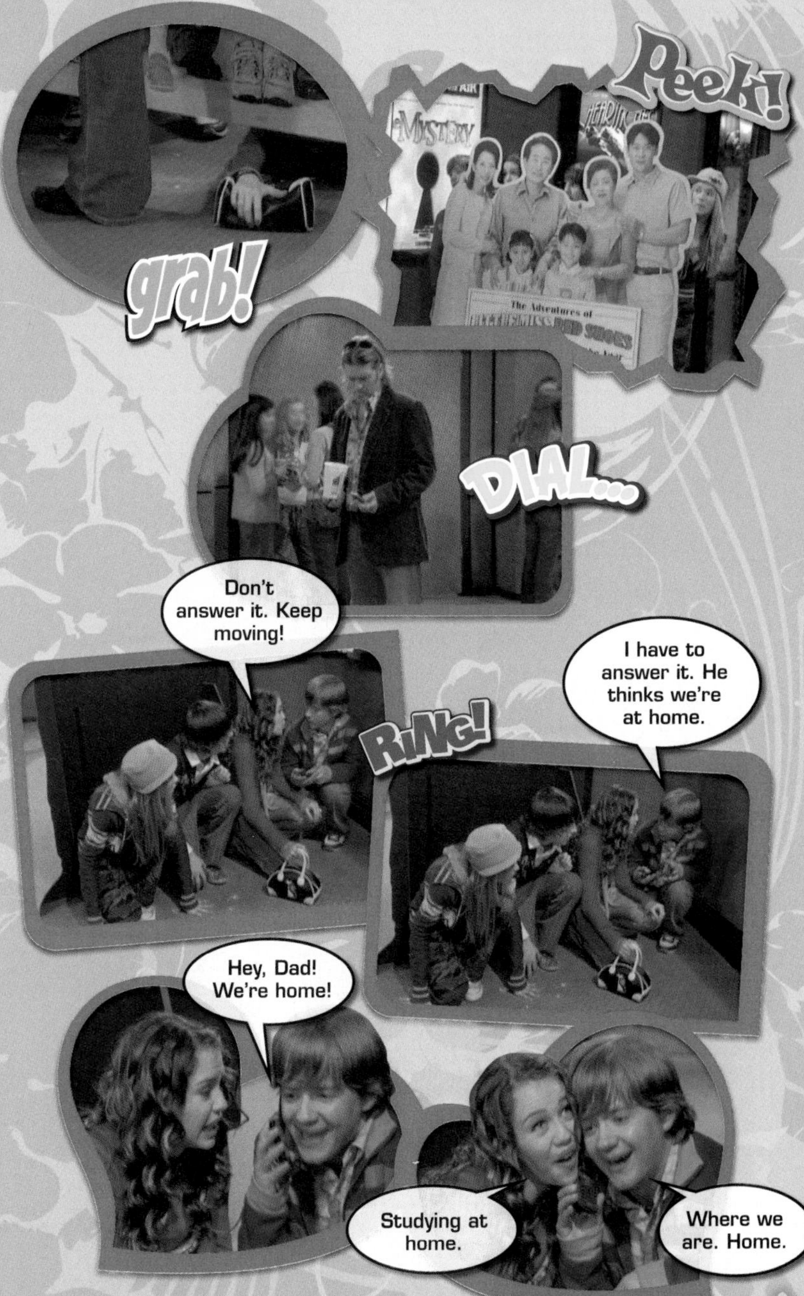
grab!
Peek!
MYSTERY
DIAL...
Don't answer it. Keep moving!
RING!
I have to answer it. He thinks we're at home.
Hey, Dad! We're home!
Studying at home.
Where we are. Home.

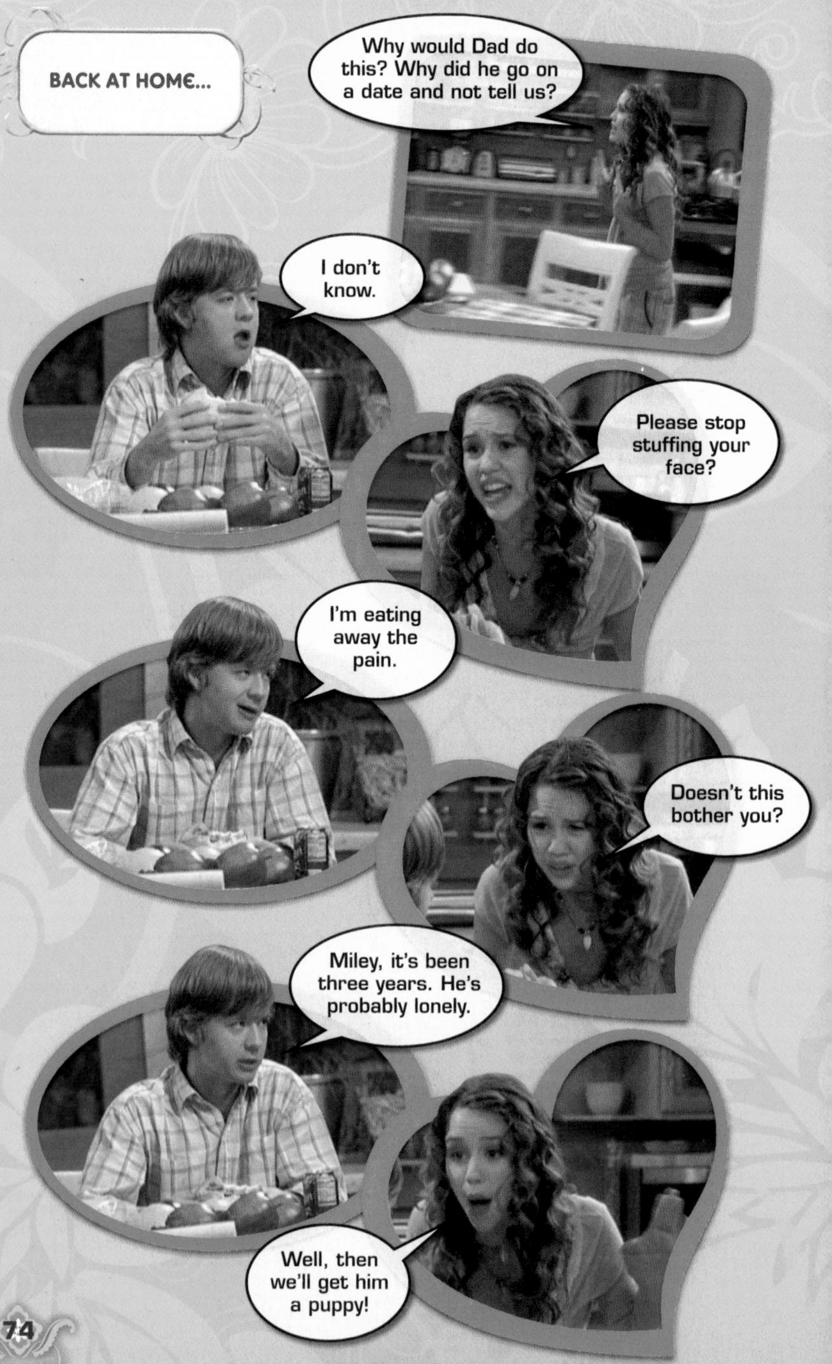
BACK AT HOME...
Why would Dad do this? Why did he go on a date and not tell us?
I don't know.
Please stop stuffing your face?
I'm eating away the pain.
Doesn't this bother you?
Miley, it's been three years. He's probably lonely.
Well, then we'll get him a puppy!

I just wish I knew something about this woman. What does she do for a living? Does she have any kids?

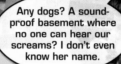

Any dogs? A sound-proof basement where no one can hear our screams? I don't even know her name.

Margo Diamond.

What?

Dad's Palm Pilot. Movie Saturday night... Margo Diamond.

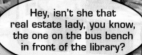

Hey, isn't she that real estate lady, you know, the one on the bus bench in front of the library?

79

Um. Hi. I'm Hannah Montana, and I'm looking for a house.
That is the stupidest thing I've ever heard!
Lady, you're not gonna sell many houses with that attitude.
Sorry. Telephone.
Hi. Ah, what a thrill to meet you. My niece is a big fan of yours.
Really? Well, how old is she? What does she look like and do you happen to have a picture of her?
Not why we're here.

85

Ah, I don't know what to say, Dad.

It was her idea. I tried to stop her. I'm just as disappointed as you are.

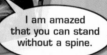

I am amazed that you can stand without a spine.

Hi. I brought you these.

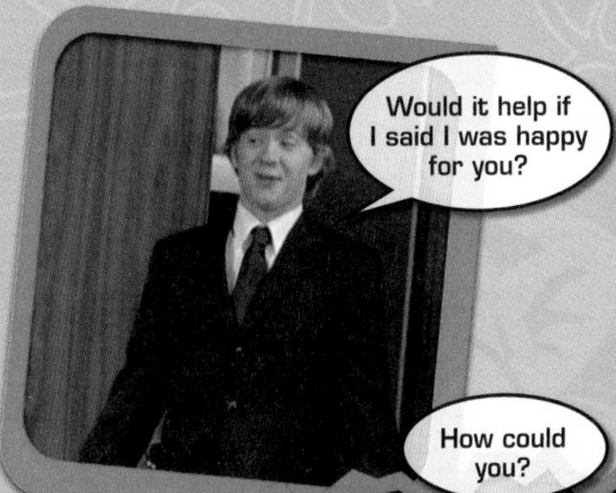
Would it help if I said I was happy for you?

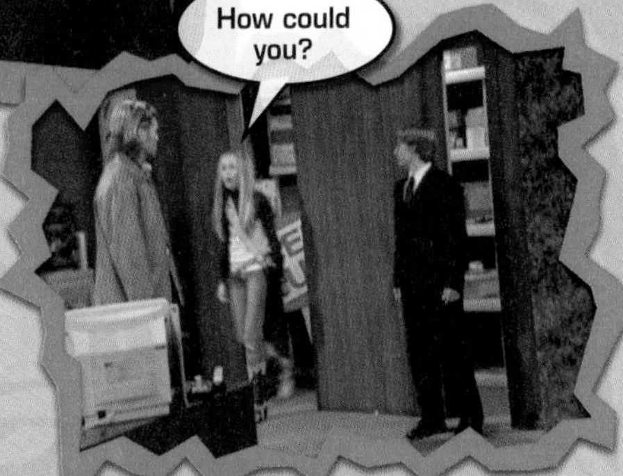
How could you?

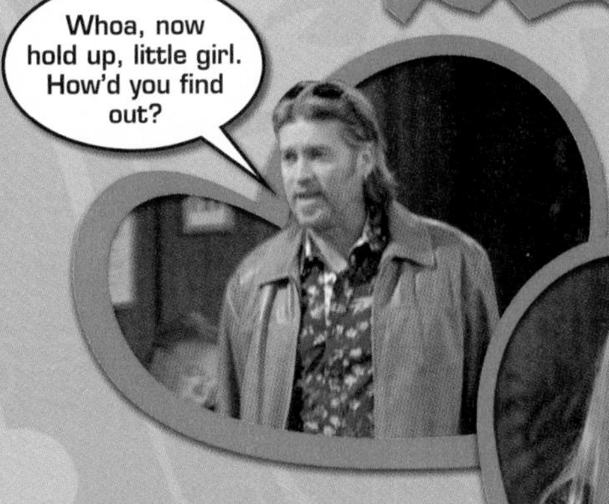
Whoa, now hold up, little girl. How'd you find out?

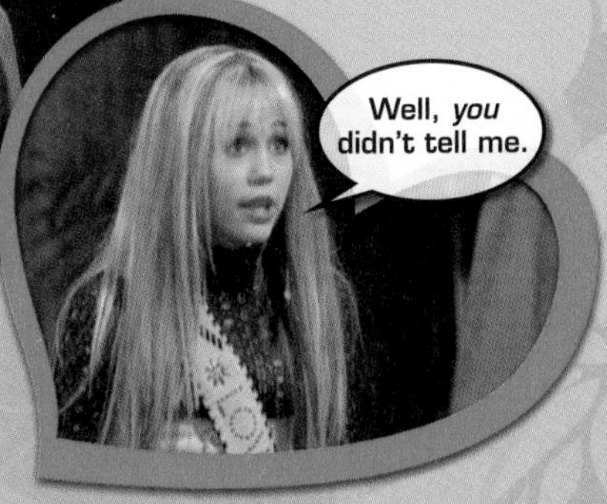
Well, *you* didn't tell me.

93

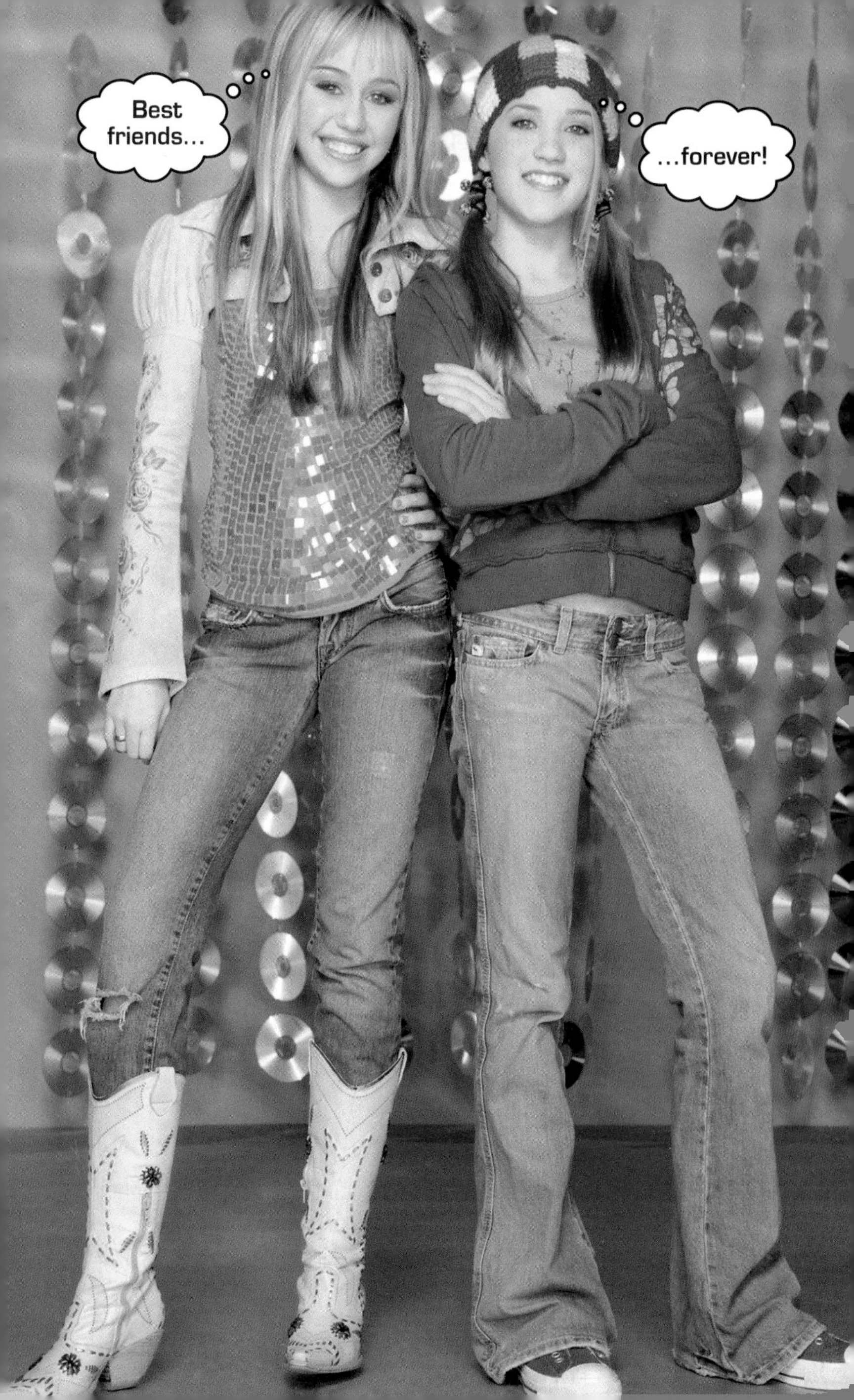
Best friends...
...forever!